FAITH AND FAKE NEWS

FAITH

&

FAKE

NEWS

A Guide to Consuming Information Wisely

RACHEL I. WIGHTMAN

William B. Eerdmans Publishing Company
Grand Rapids, Michigan

Wm. B. Eerdmans Publishing Co.
4035 Park East Court SE, Grand Rapids, Michigan 49546
www.eerdmans.com

Published 2023
Printed in the United States of America

29 28 27 26 25 24 23   1 2 3 4 5 6 7

ISBN 978-0-8028-8245-5

Library of Congress Cataloging-in-Publication Data

A catalog record for this book is available from the Library of
Congress.

For Brian, who believed in me and these ideas

And for James—I hope we are creating a better world for you

Contents

Introduction

As we started a first class about the intersection of faith and news and misinformation, I asked the participants why each of them was in the class. What drew them to give up an hour of their time each week for four weeks? Sam said he was overwhelmed by information online and it was hard to know whom and what to trust. Sally said she was a doctor and was discouraged by all the misinformation she saw online about COVID-19 and wanted to learn some tools to know how to talk with others about the misinformation. Carl said he saw so much division and wanted to learn more about what it meant to love his neighbors online. Over and over, I heard the anxieties and frustrations of people in the class:

- How do I know what to trust online and on social media?
- So much information comes at me, I find it all overwhelming.
- How do I talk with people in my life who seemingly believe conspiracy theories or misinformation, or at the very least, have opinions different from mine?
- Should I like a friend's post if I agree or disagree with it? What if I can't tell whether it's true? Will they notice or be disappointed if I *don't* like their post?

- Do I comment online when I disagree with someone or should I talk to them in person?
- I'm so overwhelmed by my social media, it's easier to disengage and not spend time trying to sort through it all. I've given up.

These comments at the beginning of class echo what I hear in casual conversation, at church, and with friends. I get a sense that there's too much division in people's personal and online lives, and people are simply overwhelmed by all that goes on in online spaces. On a deeper level, I sense anxiety and worry surrounding their time online. Maybe you resonate with those questions or have similar emotions: fear, confusion, uncertainty. So many people are overwhelmed by the world around them and the barrage of information. But there's hope—hope for us who are Christians to be salt and light in our online spaces just as much as in our physical spaces. For many, online communities have become a proxy for physical communities, and we can bring our faith to both.

I also see and hear so many people talk about how they're unsure what to trust online. I hear these comments in casual conversation, and I hear them as a librarian, at work when I talk with faculty about the research skills of their students. People read news from different sources that seem to contradict each other. We have so many choices on where to get our news and information, and we're bombarded with it when we open a browser or scroll through social media. It's hard to distinguish between credible, true information and false or manipulated information. It's hard to tell the difference between actual news and advertisements or opinion pieces parading as news.

WHY FAITH AND FAKE NEWS? AN ORIGIN STORY

A series of events in the fall of 2019 led me to the idea that teaching a class about misinformation for Christians and churches might be a good idea, or at least helpful to those in my immediate circle. In 2019, I found myself in several conversations with friends who shared their frustration with the news and online environments. They commented on how much news there was and how it seemed so divisive. At the time, the news was full of political division in the United States as we looked ahead to an election year in 2020 and heard so much polarizing information about Democrats and Republicans and the president at the time. Friends regularly told me about family members with whom they disagreed and read different news sources, but they weren't sure how to move forward in conversations with those family members. These friends recognized that many people they loved held viewpoints different from their own. They also seemed to recognize that where those loved ones got their information from was different from their own sources. But ultimately, they were unsure what to do about it or how to have productive conversations.

As I listened to my friends, I noticed how much they loved their friends and family and wanted to have conversations with them about current events. They wanted to talk about the truth of the situations and what they saw. But my friends also struggled with how to talk with loved ones about the things they saw in the world when they all disagreed so much. I remember friends telling me that it seemed like everyone was looking at the world with their own facts. In retrospect, I wonder whether they were seeing the world through the lenses of their different values. People felt misunderstood and angry, and many of my friends chose, instead, not to engage with particular topics so as not to talk about those things. When we and our loved ones see the world through different lenses, it can become harder and harder to feel like we're able to have real conversations, instead having surface-level conversations about what's happening in our world.

In the fall of 2019, I also took a class at my church on cross-cultural competence. The class focused on how to be effective in our US culture that's becoming more and more diverse. The facilitators encouraged us to think about our own biases, the spaces we regularly inhabit, and how we interact with people who come from cultures different from our own. And as they talked about bias, I couldn't help but wonder what role information plays in our biases. How does what we see online affect how we see the world and, in turn, our biases? We often think about our biases as being internal or informed by our families of origins. But as a librarian, I also thought about the information we consume and how it influences the way we see the world and the people in it. I thought about the power information has to form us and our views. I realized that we not only need to look inside ourselves to address our biases but also to our outside world and how it impacts us, particularly how our news and information sources may be trying to get us to see others in a specific way. Whether we realize it or not, news and other content creators have their own perspective, and as we consume their information, we also consume their perspective.

Finally, during a sermon series on racism and multiculturalism at my church, one of our pastors talked about the importance of checking our inputs—meaning we need to have inputs from people who are different from us in order to help us understand the world God created and the beauty of the diversity within it. At that moment I realized that people need skills and resources to check their inputs well. I knew that the information landscape is complicated and how easy it is to find bad information or get overwhelmed. I wanted to help people think critically about the information they found and help them find information that would actually encourage them to engage with new perspectives. I knew that how information is structured online impacts what we see. We don't all see the same things when we search online. So engaging with new perspectives online can actually be quite difficult because our online spaces are often echo chambers, which we'll talk about later in this book.

Our church, Mill City Church (MCC) in Minneapolis, regularly hosts classes during an "equipping hour" before the service, which seemed like the perfect venue. The classes cover topics from financial literacy to how to read the Bible to emotionally healthy spirituality, and I couldn't help but wonder whether a class on information and news literacy could be helpful. I knew people of faith needed the tools I taught college students just as much, if not more so. After procrastinating, I finally posed the topic to one of our pastors, and she agreed that it was what was needed, particularly as we looked ahead to the 2020 election year.

The class has morphed over the last few years as I've offered it to more and more churches. A global pandemic and lots of unrest here in the United States necessitated some changes to the content. The issues we talked about in 2019 have changed to some extent, although we still see lots of division in the United States, and politics continue to be a major source of news and division. When the idea first came to me, people were looking ahead to 2020 only as an election year.

Of course, 2020 changed in ways we couldn't have imagined. The first series of workshops I taught in the beginning of 2020 ended one week before the COVID-19 pandemic was declared, and at the last session, talk of coronavirus buzzed in the air. Little did we know that two weeks later, many of us would be working from home and that the world was going to change dramatically. But at its core, conversations about faith and fake news continue to have the same goals two years later as when I first initiated a conversation in 2019: to help Christians understand the information landscape, to think about how their faith intersects with their online spaces, and to help them be wise consumers of information. We consume information every day, and it shapes us in ways we may not realize. These conversations give people tools to notice the ways in which that information may be shaping them, how they may be responding, and giving them tools to respond in a more Christlike manner.

You might be wondering how this relates to my work as a librarian. That's okay—there are lots of stereotypes about librarians and what we do, and I know that not everyone completely understands the connection. As a librarian, I'm trained in teaching others about information: how to find it, how to evaluate it, and how to use it. Many librarians have a master's degree in library *and* information science. I became a librarian because I was drawn to the idea of helping people and communities engage with information. (Surprise! It actually had nothing to do with reading.) I even took classes in community informatics, which helped me think about the ways in which technology impacts communities. Prior to becoming a librarian, I also took graduate classes in community development, which prepared me to think about the ways in which communities grow and change.

Librarians connect people to information in lots of ways. Traditionally we did that via print formats, like books and newspapers, but in the last twenty years, much of our work has moved online. I've been a librarian for almost fifteen years, teaching primarily college students how to find and evaluate information. My husband, Brian, is also a librarian, although he works with medical professionals. Our house is full of conversations around how to help people find and use information. As a librarian trained in both community development and information organization and retrieval, I tend to see the world through a lens of how information is connected to people and communities, hence the way those conversations and experiences in 2019 led me to explore the intersection of faith and fake news. I already taught classes to college students on research skills, but what would it look like to teach those skills to faith communities and help them be truth-seekers and equip them to better share the truth of current situations with others? I saw another avenue in which I could equip people to be change-makers in their communities.

STARTING WITH A REFLECTION AND SCRIPTURE

Let's start with a Scripture reflection to help us all center ourselves on Jesus and loving others. Before we dive into learning about the information landscape and tools, it's helpful to pause and think about our faith and the role it might play in these spaces. This allows us to start thinking about the ways in which our faith shows up in everyday ways. This isn't about finding one right way to engage online or about finding one right answer to a current social issue. But instead, we want to find ways to practice our faith in these spaces, building faith-filled habits of applying our beliefs to our online spaces, and it can be helpful to reflect a bit on Scripture as we get started. Applying our Christian framework to our information-seeking habits allows us to live out our faith in a very practical way.

A helpful starting point is Ephesians 4:14–16, which says:

> ¹⁴Then we will no longer be immature like children. We won't be tossed and blown about by every wind of new teaching. We will not be influenced when people try to trick us with lies so clever they sound like the truth. ¹⁵Instead, we will speak the truth in love, growing in every way more and more like Christ, who is the head of his body, the church. ¹⁶He makes the whole body fit together perfectly. As each part does its own special work, it helps the other parts grow, so that the whole body is healthy and growing and full of love. (NLT)

If we were meeting in person as opposed to you reading this book, we'd spend some time reflecting on these verses in light of the idea of information and fake news. I don't use these scriptures to imply there's a right or wrong way to engage with information but rather to help center ourselves toward a posture of reflection and making connections between our faith and online spaces. I find that the willingness to step into this work—finding the connections between our faith and online environments—is more about our heart and less about a checklist of right and wrong steps to take.

As you reflect on those verses, I'll ask you some questions. If you read this book with others from your family or church, talk about these questions together.

- What stands out to you in these verses when you think about how you engage with news, information, people you know, and people you don't know?
- What does it look like to speak love in online spaces?
- Have you ever felt like you were tricked with information, into believing something you later found out to be untrue?
- How do we, as the church, reflect Jesus's love in online spaces?

I find that starting with these few verses can help us center our hearts on Jesus and how he wants the church to be one body, before we dive into practical tools or the specifics of the information landscape and algorithms and social media. If we approach these spaces with the goal of being more like Christ, we step into the spaces in a way that will be more productive, helping us find truth in current events and other areas. I've also found that these verses give us the opportunity to focus on how we connect with others as we think about being part of the whole body of the church. We can approach others in order to have meaningful conversations. One time in a class, someone remarked that it was helpful for him to remember that having a practice of fact-checking was important not only for him as an individual but also for his community, and I loved that he could see the bigger picture of it all.

These verses aren't the only ones we could look at, of course. I actually believe we can look to the Bible as a whole, at the entire narrative to see what God is doing to inform this conversation. Throughout the Bible, God reveals himself and his care for human beings, and we have the opportunity to join him in his work. My church often talks about how God wants to make the wrong things right in this world and that we get to be part of that work, too, as we find ways to partner with him and make the world a better place. I can't help but think that he would also want us to be part of finding ways to minimize false information.

These verses are also often a good starting point because online spaces can be overwhelming and we can feel like we're getting blown about by the latest conspiracy theory or political division. Instead, we're called to stand firm in who Jesus is and let him shape our character even through and in our online spaces. We can learn to speak the truth in love when we disagree with others. We can let the information we consume help us grow more like Christ. In the same way we might think about how the food we consume impacts our physical bodies, we might also think about how the ways we consume information affect our minds and hearts. And perhaps most importantly, we can be full of love when we interact with others in our online spaces.

THE INFORMATION LANDSCAPE

Now that we've centered our hearts a bit, think back over the past twenty-four hours: How many times did you use a computer or smartphone? Did you read the news? Watch a show? Text a friend? Buy something from Amazon? Scroll through a social media feed? If you're like many people in the United States (and elsewhere), you probably looked at a device more than once. Most likely more than once each hour. Over and over, we reach for our devices, and in the past twenty-five to thirty years (at least), we've seen a huge shift in our culture as our use of these devices and the internet has grown. From shopping to learning about current events to attending school to communicating with our friends and family, we use the internet in many aspects of our lives. In the last day alone, I've used the internet and my phone to video call with my family, order groceries and takeout for dinner, check my email, watch a show, play an online game, look up a restaurant, and probably more things I'm forgetting.

In the past, we might have done those things in person or in some other physical format. For example, we might have gone to a store, called a friend, read a physical newspaper or book, played a board game, watched a show on a TV, talked to a neighbor. In the past, our physical community was often our greatest source of information. The changes we've seen in our culture in the last few decades are outstanding and noteworthy. The effects of technology and the internet on the economy, our education systems, and our communication methods aren't hard to see. But as a librarian, the effect I'm most interested in is the way we engage with information. From news to school assignments to googling our latest medical symptom, we use the internet to meet many of our information needs.

What do I mean by this? Every day you look for and engage with information. From reading or watching the news to looking up the menu of your favorite restaurant to watching videos on YouTube or TikTok, you engage with information in hundreds of ways. We don't necessarily think about our online habits in terms of information, but that's what we do: find and use information. The *Merriam-Webster* dictionary defines "information" as "knowledge obtained from investigation, study, or instruction." In our online spaces, we often obtain knowledge, even if that knowledge is simply finding the hours of the local grocery store or looking up a movie review.

As all these changes have taken place in our culture and we've turned to the internet for our information needs, I also see and hear people express growing uncertainty about what they can or should trust online. They were saying this in 2019 when I first had the idea to offer a workshop, and I still hear people say that in 2022, as I write this. People read or hear news from different sources that seem to contradict each other. Or they find news stories that are really opinion pieces or advertisements parading as news, which makes their time online more confusing. We have so many choices on where to get our news and information. We're bombarded with it when we open a browser or scroll through social media. We get decision fatigue trying to decide where to go for information or trying to figure out whether something is trustworthy. It's getting harder to distinguish between credible information and unreliable information. It all looks the same on a screen and can be hard to tell the difference.

At the same time that we get overwhelmed by everything we see online and on social media, we also see more and more division in our culture and our relationships. We see it in our families as we struggle to talk through issues with the ones we love the most. Our churches, too, see the division as we sort through the issues we see in our world. It's evident by the comments we see on social media and in our everyday conversations. It doesn't take us long to see how much division there is in our culture, churches, homes, workplaces. For example, during the COVID-19 pandemic, people posted and shared opinions on everything from wearing masks to getting vaccines to remote school options. The science behind decisions changed over time, causing further confusion. During the unrest following the killing of George Floyd in Minneapolis in 2020, we saw all kinds of comments about policing, racism, and more. For many people, the division is exacerbated when different groups follow different experts and can't seem to agree on who is actually right on the issue.

The information landscape is complex and confusing. It has provided us with lots of conveniences—online shopping, video calls to connect with loved ones, and easy access to current events—but it has also created spaces that are overwhelming, not just for people of faith but for everyone. As Christians, we have an opportunity to engage differently in these online spaces. If we want to be light in dark places, we'll need to examine our online spaces and reflect on our own behaviors and habits to see how our faith shows up in these places. But before we ask *how* our faith shows up, we need to ask ourselves, "*Does* our faith show up?"

SOME BASIC CONCEPTS

Before we get too far, let's define some terms. What do I mean by "online spaces"? Online spaces are any places where you show up and use the internet (note that there's overlap in many of these)—for example:

- email
- social media, such as Instagram, Facebook, Twitter, TikTok, and Snapchat
- YouTube and other media platforms
- news coverage—reading or watching
- general websites and blogs
- online gaming.

More and more of these spaces are accessed via our smartphones, although not all of them for everyone. And for many of us, they started on our computers. Some of us can remember the days of dial-up internet, when online spaces felt new and exciting. But regardless of where or how you access the internet, in all these spaces, we have a choice: We can passively scroll, watch, and consume, or we can pay attention, invite the Spirit, and use these spaces in our work of joining God in making the wrong things right. When we pray the Lord's Prayer, we ask that God's kingdom would come down on earth as it is in heaven. It's worth exploring what it looks like for us to bring God's kingdom into our online spaces just as much as our physical spaces.

It's also worth noting that the internet is a complex space. It isn't the same as the dial-up wonder some of us remember of the 1990s. Back then we logged on to the internet to check email, websites were much more basic and static, and content like chat rooms and online gaming were in their infancy. Now the internet is a complex intersection of both our broadband and Wi-Fi connections and our 4G or 5G cell phone connections. The internet is the intersection of websites and blogs that people create on their own, apps that allow us to read the news, track our water intake, read the Bible, and watch TV shows. The internet allows scientists and doctors to publish their findings, celebrities to post videos, politicians to reach their constituents, chefs to share recipes, and more. It's complex and not simply one thing that contains one kind of information.

Two other terms that are often used and left undefined are "misinformation" and "disinformation." Both can be found in all those online spaces. Both are problematic. But it's important to know the difference. Misinformation is information that's out of context or incorrect, or both. It's easy to share and can circulate easily in online spaces. Disinformation is also false information but intentionally so. It can also circulate easily online and shows up in all our online spaces. These two terms, while they may be used interchangeably, are actually quite different, as the intention behind them isn't the same. We'll talk more later about how to identify false information, but for now, know that these terms matter. We want to be clear when we talk about controversial topics, and knowing whether something is misinformation or disinformation is an important distinction.

I've been told that I overspiritualize these topics, that maybe this is all a bit too much. Does Jesus really care about what we post on social media? Or whether we retweet that news article on Twitter? Does Jesus care whether we accidentally share misinformation on our Facebook page or Instagram?

He does. Jesus was a truth-teller; he confronted injustice, and he loved the marginalized and vulnerable. He wanted people to see the truth of who he is and how he was bringing the kingdom of God near to those he met. He taught us to love our neighbors and to be a good Samaritan. As we engage on social media, we, too, have an opportunity to speak the truth to others. Sharing misinformation unintentionally or disinformation intentionally isn't a part of Jesus's truth-telling kingdom. Instead, we have an opportunity to pay attention to what the Holy Spirit might teach us and where we're led in our online spaces. Do we pay attention to the Spirit's promptings when we use our social media apps, or do we get sucked into the shiny technology as we passively consume content? What's the posture of our hearts in these spaces? Do we approach our online spaces with an intent to prove ourselves right and others wrong or to learn from others? We have an opportunity to be like Jesus, who knew the truth about people and our world and still responded with kindness, by listening, and by asking questions.

Not only do we have an opportunity to be more like Jesus and to listen to the Spirit's promptings when we're online, but also our actions on social media and online give us an opportunity to love our neighbors well. We talk about loving our neighbors in church all the time: making a meal for a neighbor who just had a baby, running an errand for a friend who had surgery, donating to the local homeless shelter. All of these are good things.

But what does it look like to love your neighbors in your online spaces? Here's another way to think about this: What would the Holy Spirit think about your online interactions and engagement? What's the posture of your heart as you enter into these spaces? Do you speak truth into your online spaces, and do you respect others and love the marginalized like Jesus did? (Yes, it's possible to do these things online, although sometimes it feels impossible.) Our online culture is full of sound bites—quick comments, likes, tweets, and shares. It can be easy to lose sight of the people behind the posts. When simply looking at words on a screen, we forget that the person that posted them has a story and is made in the image of God. We can lose sight of the deeper connections with others; a lot can get lost in the few sentences of a social media post.

We'll discuss this more later, but, in the meantime, think about who are your online neighbors and community. Who do you interact with on social media? After learning some practical tools for fact-checking and seeking truth, we'll explore the idea of caring about our online neighbors more. In the meantime, think about the last interaction you had with someone online (liked their photo, retweeted, etc.). Was your interaction loving? Was it kind? By loving and kind, I think about the characteristics of love listed in 1 Corinthians 13:4-5: patient, not boastful, not proud, not keeping a record of wrongs. This doesn't mean we allow others to believe misinformation. But do your online interactions reflect loving responses?

LOOKING AHEAD

If Christians want to be salt and light in our world, we need to understand and engage mindfully and intentionally in these online spaces, inviting the Holy Spirit into this part of our lives. But first, we need to understand the big picture and how the information landscape is structured. Then we need to use tools to evaluate the information and news we find. Finally, once we've evaluated the information, we can intentionally choose how we engage with others, in order to love our neighbors, friends, and family and to share truth with them.

It's not easy to talk about these things. We're generally used to passively consuming content and information, scrolling on our phones or online. Or sometimes we get focused on the issues themselves instead of on how we engage with the information—how to find the information on the issues. Sometimes I don't want to be objective about information or what I see or hear online. I see something I disagree with and get angry before actually noticing where the information came from. It's easier to see the person who posted it as the other, villainizing not only their opinion but the person themself. But what I've found is that the more we let the Holy Spirit into our online spaces, the more chances we have to become like Jesus. To think outside ourselves, to engage with new information, and to love others.

The Holy Spirit can also help us determine which parts of our online culture to pay attention to. With so much information at our fingertips, it can feel like many different issues and news stories compete for our attention—because they do! We can feel that if we don't pay attention to X, Y, or Z issues or read the right news source, we don't engage correctly with the world around us. I've heard people talk about the guilt or shame of not being able to keep up. We'll explore this more as we talk about the information landscape, but this is another area the Holy Spirit can help us with—learning to pay attention to the things God wants us to pay attention to. We can't read all the news stories or invest money in every issue. It takes the whole church body to do those things, and as we engage with our online spaces, the Holy Spirit can prompt us to pay attention to specific things.

As you go through this book, you'll learn more about how online spaces work and how the information landscape is structured. We'll talk about strategies you can use to evaluate what you see, hear, and read. We'll look at strategies for connecting with others in this divisive time and discerning how to move forward with the information you do find. Most importantly, we'll think about how our faith intersects with all these things. You'll be challenged to look beyond the issues themselves but at the information that describes the issues. You'll be prompted to see past your own opinions and to honestly engage with sources and news that you might disagree with. It's not about whether you watch liberal or conservative media or about which specific news sources you follow but rather about how we engage with information we find on a deeper level.

In the last few years, as I've taught more classes and done more research on the intersection of faith and information, I've found that people often assume I approach these concepts from the same side they do, specifically their political side. If someone has a conservative political point of view, they assume I'm going to share conservative news sources as the best Christian resources. And vice versa for those that have a more liberal political viewpoint.

Sometimes people also ask me, "But do the people who *need* your class actually come?" which usually means, "Do the people who have opinions opposite to mine come to the class so they can learn the right things?" The reality is it's neither about conservative or liberal political viewpoints nor about who needs the class (we all do!) but instead about being thoughtful and intentional in how we engage with information on current social and political and other topics. Faith and Fake News classes and this book come out of a place of wanting to help the church think about the ways in which our faith and online spaces intersect, encouraging us all to engage more carefully and mindfully.

Practically speaking, each chapter of this book will discuss a different aspect of the information landscape and skills we can use to navigate more thoughtfully online. Each chapter will also include a list of reflection questions you can use to help you think a bit deeper on the topics covered. There are no right or wrong answers with these questions, but rather they offer a chance for you to reflect on your own habits online and think a bit deeper than just which social media or news platforms you follow. Taking stock of what we already do will help us decide how we move forward. Discuss your answers with trusted friends and family to further solidify your reflections. I've also included a list of additional resources with each chapter if you'd like to learn from additional experts on these topics. These resources come from a variety of experts in different fields: psychology, technology, and journalism. Some are from a Christian perspective and some are not. They're listed to give you a chance to learn more on the topics discussed from others who have spent years researching them.

Each chapter also contains at least one exercise you can use to help you apply what you learn, to help you put into practice and take time to reflect on new concepts. It's easy to breeze by something new and think, "I'd like to try that," but then not actually follow through. Like the reflection questions, the exercises for each chapter don't have right or wrong answers but will walk you through some steps to help you engage more fully and reflect on where you might be called to take steps in your own life. Think of these exercises as miniexperiments. My church in Minneapolis focuses a lot on experiments, and I've found it to be a helpful framework for trying new things. An experiment allows us to try something, reflect on it, and ask God what direction might be next. The exercises in this book are just that—a chance for you to try something and pay attention to what God might be saying to you. Use them to reflect on your behaviors and habits in online spaces or to try something new. Like the reflection questions, consider sharing your experience with a small group or partner or friend to help hold you accountable to both trying the exercise and following through with any changes you want to make.

Again, this book isn't designed to convince you of a certain political ideology or to change your mind on a particular issue. Although we'll use current issues and events as examples, the goal is to help you evaluate where you get information about those issues. This book will give you a chance to reflect on how and where you get information and how you engage with it. For example, some questions you may encounter are the following: Do you passively scroll through Twitter and let that inform your views, or do you intentionally seek out experts on the issues?

And how do you know that they're experts? Do you have a few steps you can use to check the information you hear? When you engage on issues, do you look at only one side? Do you know how to find the other side(s)? So many current issues are often less black and white and more gray. Learning to be wise online involves learning to look for the gray.

My goal as a librarian and in this book isn't to convince people to change their minds on a particular topic or issue but to help them think about how to engage with those issues more broadly. Librarians connect people to information and teach others how to find and use information. As a Christian, I find it so important to also focus on loving our neighbors even when those neighbors may have lifestyles, ideas, or cultures different from our own. The ideas in this book live at the overlap of these two things. My goal is to help you be a wise consumer of information, a consumer that's guided both by practical tools for navigating online spaces and by the Holy Spirit.

The concepts in this book aren't a list of the best and worst news sources. It's not written to make you stop using the internet or to be afraid of what you see. Instead, this book is a space where I hope you'll be challenged to think about the ways in which your faith shows up (or not) in what you do online. You'll learn more about the information landscape, about how things work online, and how you see what you see in your online spaces. We'll define some terms, we'll learn some practical tools for fact-checking, we'll challenge some of our biases by seeing the biases in our online spaces, and perhaps most importantly, we'll reflect on our faith and how we let the Holy Spirit influence us in our online spaces.

It can feel a bit scary to let go of what you know or to be willing to learn something new. But what I've found in life is that the scary things are generally the ones worth doing—the ones that make me more like Jesus.

REFLECTION QUESTIONS

- Reflect on the different areas you consume information. Where do you spend your online time? Social media, TV news, Google?
    - How much of that information do you purposely seek out and go to directly?
    - How much of that information do you consume passively, that is, simply by scrolling online or on a smartphone?
- Which apps do you use on your phone? Instagram? TikTok? Facebook? Something else? How much time do you spend in each app? (Most smartphones have a tracker in the settings that allows you to see how much time you spend in each app.)
- Whom might you consider your online neighbors? With whom do you regularly interact online? (Or consume their information?) Are they people you know in real life or people you simply follow on social media? We'll revisit these questions again later, but it's helpful to start reflecting on these things as we start these conversations.
- What's our role as Christians in a world full of easy-to-access information?
- Why should we be critical of the information we consume? Why do *you* want to be critical of the information you consume?
- How do we let the information we consume inform our faith? How do we use the lens of our faith to interpret the information?
- Or do we let our faith and the Holy Spirit inform how we interpret the information we consume?
- How do you bring your Christian identity into these spaces? Will you look at information differently because you're a Christian? What's your invitation from the Holy Spirit?
- How does your identity as a Christian shape the way you approach your online behavior and habits? What about the fruit of the Spirit?

- When you hop on social media, what are your goals? Pay attention. Do you scroll because you're bored? Do you try to connect with others? The reason we find ourselves online can be an indicator of our current state of being and help us decide whether we want to make changes moving forward.

PART ONE

The Information Landscape

The following framework contains three main steps for being a wise consumer of information:

1. Understand the information landscape.
2. Evaluate the information you find, see, read, or hear.
3. Choose and discern how you want to engage with the information, including:
   a. loving your (online) neighbors and speaking truth to other people and those who believe misinformation;
   b. practicing humility in learning new perspectives.

These are the main topics in our journeys to being more mindful and intentional in our communities, relationships, and online spaces. In this first section, chapters 1–3, we'll tackle the first step: understanding the information landscape. In later sections, we'll learn more about evaluating information and how to engage with it. But for now, we'll focus on the big picture. This extraordinarily massive, and for some people overwhelming, landscape contains news, videos, images, and opinions constantly bombarding us. It's something we're immersed in but don't always know much about how it works, beyond a few basics. But understanding our online world is key to moving forward intentionally and mindfully as we interact in new ways online. I know this information landscape can be stressful, and I hope the content in this book will give you language to talk about what you see online. Like many things in life, the more we can name and understand the things we find overwhelming, the less stressful they become.

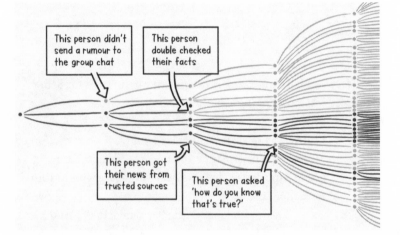

Illustration of how individuals can address misinformation to limit its spread. Created by Toby Morris and Siouxsie Wiles, copyright 2020, CC-BY-SA 4.0.

As we start this journey of intersecting our faith with fact-checking, I've found the graphic above to help us think about where we're headed. At the beginning of the pandemic, this graphic was created to help people think about how or whether their information habits relating to COVID-19 contributed to the spread of misinformation. The creators used the term "infodemic," which the World Health Organization defines as "too much information including false or misleading information in digital and physical environments during a disease outbreak. It causes confusion and risk-taking behaviours that can harm health. It also leads to mistrust in health authorities and undermines the public health response."[1] While this was originally designed to focus specifically on health information, many of us would agree that it's not just health information that falls within a "too much information" category; we see too much information on all kinds of topics, and this graphic is helpful to demonstrate the deluge of information we find ourselves in.

But what I also like about this graphic is the reminder that we have a choice about what we do online. We don't have to passively scroll through social media, consume without thinking, or share false information. As we'll see throughout this book and in this particular section, misinformation spreads in many ways, some of which are out of our control. But this graphic reminds us that some things *are* in our control. This graphic reminds us that while the platforms are big—and admittedly have their own work to do to combat misinformation—we also have a role and can make changes to how we engage online. Jesus doesn't want us to be part of sharing misinformation. We have the power to make choices in how we engage, and in doing so, we get to be part of slowing the spread of false information. What better place for Christians to be situated than in stopping the spread of misinformation and spreading truth instead?

CHAPTER 1

Algorithms and Filter Bubbles

Have you ever tried searching for something and later saw ads for it on your social media? Or shopped at an online store that you later saw lots of ads for? Often in Faith and Fake News classes, someone mentions their frustration at how they feel when ads follow them online. I hear about this in my personal conversations, too, not just in classes I teach. I've heard friends or students call this phenomenon everything from annoying to creepy. Maybe you feel the same way. Just recently, I visited a website for a company that sold pots and pans, and later when I checked my email, I saw a "Thank you for subscribing to our newsletter" email from the same company, even though I never typed in my email address for them. Weird and very unnerving because somehow the company knew to connect my browsing their website to my email address. And sure enough, I've been getting emails from them regularly since then. I really need to click on "unsubscribe."

This phenomenon we see in so many places online is due, primarily, in part to the structure and personalization of our online spaces. Many of us use social media, Google, and other sites but don't necessarily understand how the platforms work together, how they decide what to show us, or how they're connected. Or sometimes we know only the basics. My goal is always to start conversations about fact-checking by giving people an understanding about how information is structured and to help people understand why they see certain content in online spaces. Once they have a basic understanding of how their online spaces are structured, we can talk about fact-checking or verifying information and what to do about it.

ALGORITHMS

What do we mean by the "information landscape"? As mentioned in the introduction, it refers to the types of spaces we inhabit online, on our phones, mobile devices, and on our computers. These spaces consist of websites, social media platforms, streaming video platforms, and more. Together these create a landscape that we navigate every day and one that we aren't always sure how to move through or don't realize we *are* moving through. And understanding the information landscape often starts with first understanding something called algorithms.

The basic definition of an algorithm from *Merriam-Webster* is "a process or set of rules to be followed in calculations or other problem-solving operations, especially by a computer."[1] In other words, algorithms are the computer programing behind many websites, including Google, Facebook, Instagram, and more. They use data and online behavior (yours, as well as others') to predict what you might like to see next on your social media as you browse content or in your Google or other search engine results. These algorithms—the way much of the internet is structured—take previous, or past, data to inform what you'll see in the future.

Where do these platforms get this data and behavior? As you consume information, the platforms also consume *your* information. Free doesn't always mean free when we give up some of our own data to use the platforms. To put it bluntly, we give a lot of data away when we're online or on social media. Search engines, social media platforms, websites, and more collect data as you browse, search, and spend time online. This data may include the following:

- your browser, such as Chrome, Microsoft Edge, or Safari
- your search engine, such as Google
- your operating system, such as Android or Apple
- your geographic location
- your search terms
- what you've clicked on
- a host of other data points.

The sites, platforms, and apps then use all this data to predict what types of content you might like to see or interact with next. They might predict which ad to show you next or which video on YouTube you should watch next or even what websites might show up at the top of your Google search results. It's also important to note that not all sites or platforms disclose *what* data they collect or how they use or share it. These algorithms are proprietary and part of their business models, and few companies disclose the specifics. They may even portray this personalization as in your best interest because you get to see content that's relevant to *you*. These algorithms keep you looking at their sites and, if we're honest, might get you to buy something. Or, the longer you look at a site, the more ads you might see, which is more money to the platform or website. Either way, it's usually about money.

　　This type of personalization is often presented in a positive light by these companies and platforms as something that's good for you as you get to see more content you like. You might have noticed this if you use any streaming video platforms, such as Netflix or Hulu or Disney+. If you have a profile set up in the platform and someone else in your household also has a profile, you may see that you each have slightly different recommendations based on what you've watched in the past. The platform is predicting what you'd like to see next based on what you've watched in the past. For example, my husband and I like to watch a show called *The Rookie* on Hulu, and because it's a police show, we're often shown other police or law enforcement or crime shows as suggested next shows to watch. Or, if you were to log in to our Netflix account and look at the shows recommended under my profile, you'd see a very different set of shows compared to those under my husband's profile. All thanks to personalization.

We'll talk more about why this might be problematic, but there are some helpful outcomes from this. Of course, you get personalized videos recommended on your Netflix queue, which isn't all bad for some guilty pleasure watching. You also get personalized Target coupons or Amazon recommendations, which don't feel all bad all the time either. Once, in a Faith and Fake News class, a woman remarked how much she liked personalized Target coupons, and everyone in the class could all agree that they *were* helpful. Maybe you can think of brands or stores you've tried because of this kind of targeted advertising—brands you might not have tried otherwise but now enjoy. I don't want to completely demonize all of the online personalization we see, because I know there are some benefits.

However, on the other hand, there are some drawbacks. First, these algorithms create what are sometimes called "filter bubbles." This term was coined by Eli Pariser in 2011 in his book *The Filter Bubble: How the New Personalized Web Is Changing What We Read and How We Think* and his TED talk "Beware Online Filter Bubbles." Although originating over ten years ago, this concept is still highly relevant. The term refers to the ways in which algorithms prevent us from all seeing the same things in our online spaces and how they limit what we do see through that personalization. The *Merriam-Webster* dictionary defines the term as "an environment and especially an online environment in which people are exposed only to opinions and information that conform to their existing belief."[2] Sometimes people also talk about these filter bubbles being echo chambers where we see only ourselves and others like us, echoing and hearing the same sentiments and opinions over and over.

How does this happen? As we each perform our own searches or engage with our social media on our own devices, we begin to feed the algorithms' data and in turn create filter bubbles in which we all start to see different things, personalized to ourselves and our previous searches. In his TED talk in 2011, Pariser remarked, "And what's in your filter bubble depends on who you are, and it depends on what you do. But the thing is that you don't decide what gets in. And more importantly, you don't actually see what gets edited out."[3] He describes having friends perform the same search online with different results, demonstrating that we all get personalized results online, but we also miss a lot of content without ever knowing it. And by missing out on information, we miss out on the opportunity to get a more nuanced view of the world and the events that happen around us. This limited view makes us less able to understand current events but more importantly hinders us from connecting with others and potentially from understanding their viewpoint.

Recently, I've also seen apps on my phone or websites that allow you to select or further personalize your experience or even the option to opt out of personalization. But often when you try to reduce the personalization, you'll get a warning basically reminding you that your results will be less of what you really want to see. It's presented as if the personalization is best for *you* as you're in these online spaces, using these platforms. But the reality is that removing some of the personalization doesn't benefit the *company*, because they (the company or platform) will see less of what you do or like. Without seeing your preferences, the company can't continue to show you personalized ads, which is where many of them get their funding. Again, to a large extent, this all comes down to money.

Let's pause for a second and let this sink in. What you see online is different from what I see, even if we search for the exact same thing. You might be thinking, "Great, I get to see more of what I like." But let's think about the bigger picture of what personalization might be doing for us as a society, for our relationships, and for ourselves. If you don't see the same thing as your friend when you explore online spaces, how might that impact the way the two of you see the world or current issues? When you talk with others about current issues and events, do you notice that you approach the issue from opposite or different sides? It could be that you simply disagree or have different values, but it might also be related to the fact that you both see different content in your online spaces. It's even possible one of you has seen misinformation on the topic and is responding to that.

Think about the people in your life and specifically those with whom you sometimes disagree. Can you think of a time that approaching an issue differently or talking about a current event affected one of your relationships? Could that be from the two of you literally seeing different information online or getting your news from different sources? Have you ever asked someone where they got their information from? Not in an accusatory way but in a way that invites conversation. It's no surprise to me that we see so much division in our relationships, culture, and world when our online spaces potentially provide us all with different information, tailored specifically to us. As I mentioned in the introduction, a series of events led me to this "aha!" moment, noticing the connection between the information we consume and the division we see around us. As a librarian who's trained to look at information, I couldn't help but see the intersection of our information-seeking habits with our own biases, resulting in a lot of disruption and frustration in our relationships.

I've seen this in my own relationships as I've disagreed with family and friends and realized later that we had literally seen different information on the same topic. Even during the pandemic, I often found myself in conversations with loved ones where they seemed less concerned or aware about a certain development. When I visited the news sites I know they frequent, that development wasn't discussed at all. And while a lot of this disagreement can be attributed to the differences in our news sources, there's also something to be said for the differences in our values. Even the types of news sources we value speak to how we see the world. Our values impact the way we interpret data and current events. Although a lot of disagreements stem from different information, those disagreements also stem from different sets of values.

Additionally, what does this mean for those of us who are people of faith? For Christians who want to love our neighbors and engage with the world around us? How do we engage with the world around us if others see a different reality or different perspectives in their online spaces? (And again, our online spaces take up a lot of space in our time, mind, etc.) Is it any wonder we see so much division around us if we all see different realities online?

As Christians, many of us want to be part of loving others well and sharing the hope of who God is with them. We're part of God's kingdom to pursue justice as he invites us into his work of loving the least of these. But this can be challenging when we all literally see different things online and our online spaces are where we spend a lot of time. It can be difficult when our values bump into others' values concerning how we pursue and interpret information. What looks like pursuing justice to one person may not look the same to another, making it difficult to know what to say or do. The very way people engage with current social injustices and issues may be different because they see different information about those issues. I don't think we can downplay the impact of our online spaces on ourselves and those around us.

It's a lot to take in and process, honestly. Algorithms aren't, of course, the only reason we see division in our world, but they contribute to it. The internet is a huge part of our culture and environment. Again, it takes up a lot of our time. For those of us with the financial means, we're online almost all the time. And how much of that time is influenced simply by the last things we looked at or looked up? And again, even more importantly, if we all see personalized results, what does that do to our relationships?

I've found over and over that people of faith try so hard to engage kindly with their loved ones, family, and friends. But the last few years have been difficult. In early 2020, an organization called Project Information Literacy released a study called "Information Literacy in the Age of Algorithms: Student Experiences with News and Information and the Need for Change," which looked at algorithms and how they are perceived by college students. Although the study focuses on college students, it is a fascinating look at how algorithms affect so many aspects of our online environment. In particular, the authors created a graphic that outlines the steps that take us from how our data is collected online to the division we see around us. I've included the source of the graphic in the list of additional resources at the end of this chapter if you'd like to take a look. Our culture is impacted by our online spaces, and the more we can see the connections between the two, the more easily we can make our culture more unified—or at least more understanding.

I'd encourage you to pause again right here and think about all this for a few minutes. Think about the division you see around you, and be curious. Could it be partly from the ways in which we look for information? I find that I'm less likely to villainize others in my life with whom I disagree when I think about the information they consume as different from what I consume. I've specifically asked people about where they get their news— not in the middle of a heated argument type of way, but I might say, "Hey, I'm trying to diversify my news intake. Where do you get your news from?" Often their news sources are very different from my own, and by trying to be curious about their news consumption, I can better understand the people in my life.

If you want to take this exercise a step further, do the experiment Eli Pariser mentions in his TED talk: Ask a few friends or family members to tell you about their search results on a current issue or topic. (Make sure you all use the same search terms!) Compare what they see to what you see. Or ask a friend what types of ads they've seen in their social media lately. You'll likely find some differences worth reflecting on.

ALGORITHMS, MISINFORMATION, AND BIAS

In addition to the ways in which algorithms contribute to division, all these algorithms also contribute to a couple of additional, problematic aspects of our online spaces. First, the misinformation we see online can also be proliferated through these spaces and how they're designed. The algorithms not only limit what you and I see online, but they can also add to the amount of false information we see right now. Much of the content you see online is emotionally charged. This keeps you engaged and on the platforms. Not surprisingly, false information is also often emotionally charged. This keeps people clicking on it, watching it, and sharing it. The more that people interact with false information (past data), the more it's shown online (future suggestions).

Another lesser talked about but equally important aspect of these algorithms is that they aren't neutral. Many researchers and academics look at the bias coded directly within our online algorithms. It's somewhat complicated, but algorithms are created by human beings. Human beings have bias (implicit and explicit), and that bias becomes a part of the algorithms as they're created, whether intentionally or unintentionally. Researchers explore the role in which algorithms exhibit bias and things like racism or oppression. As Christians and people who want to, I assume, be part of God's work of setting the captives free (Luke 4:18), this is also something to be aware of. The more we understand the way in which these platforms rely on algorithms to work, the more we can use them and engage online wisely and productively.

In the documentary *Coded Bias*, researchers show how facial recognition software exhibits racism by not recognizing people of color as easily as white or Caucasian faces. And yet, facial recognition software is used as part of algorithmically run artificial intelligence (AI) platforms in many different scenarios. Similarly, the book *Algorithms of Oppression* outlines the ways in which different search terms result in different, biased results in search engines. These are just two examples of the ways in which people study how bias in algorithms impacts what we see online.

Obviously, we can't blame all misinformation or disinformation or bias on algorithms. We all have a part to play, which is the exact thing we're talking about in this book. But knowing these other pieces may also help you recognize the bigger picture of the information landscape. It's not just one thing that causes false information to spread but a combination of many things that makes navigating these spaces complex.

NOW WHAT?

So how do you know whether you're in a filter bubble? How do we get out of these filter bubbles? Can we get out? Should we? Remember, filter bubbles generally focus your online content to things that confirm what you already believe.

We can and we should try to get outside our filter bubbles. But it takes quite a bit of intentionality. Much of the rest of this book describes countercultural behavior in online spaces that will help us think outside our own bubbles. In the same way, Jesus was countercultural by encouraging his followers to look after children and widows and by associating with sinners and tax collectors. The ways of Jesus were often countercultural but also reflect his love for humans and bringing the kingdom of God to earth. We can also find ways to practice being countercultural in all areas of our lives, including online. We can find ways to resist the pull of mindless scrolling and sharing of misinformation and instead use these spaces to love others well and to shine a light on the things that aren't part of God's kingdom.

The algorithms that control our online spaces thrive on passive scrolling and clicking, as they take stock of what we do and pass it on to our next interactions. Our online spaces and social media apps can consume our time and take away from having personal relationships in the real world. Instead, what if we were more intentional with our time online and with what we click on and look at? For example, what if instead of letting our social media passively feed us our news, we intentionally choose to go to specific news sites, staying in control of where we specifically get our news? (We'll talk about some ways to find alternative news sources in later chapters.)

Jesus calls us to live in our world, yes, but to also live counterculturally. He loved the marginalized and told us to care for widows and orphans. If these algorithms have the ability to keep the marginalized marginalized, to reinforce racism, to perpetrate other injustices, or to create an us-versus-them mentality, what would it look like to intentionally find ways to turn these things upside down and to engage differently online?

Now, if we're not computer programmers, there might not be a lot we can do at a large scale. I get that. But there are people working on these issues at large scale—talking with corporations, government, and so on and advocating for change. Organizations like the Center for Humane Technology or the Algorithmic Justice League advocate for larger scale measures to address many of these issues. And in the meantime, we can also work within our own spheres of influence to make changes. We can choose to make changes for ourselves and to support the large-scale work others are doing.

Later chapters in this book will give you tools to be more intentional in your online spaces, whether it's with how you research and fact-check or how you respond to others. Let's make a commitment to be Jesus in our online spaces in the same ways we try to love others in our physical spaces. Let's remember that there's a bigger picture beyond our individual social media feeds that impacts us, our relationships, and our world.

REFLECTION QUESTIONS

- As you think back over your online habits from the past week, can you identify any bubbles you might have ended up in? (See exercise 1.1 to practice noticing or identifying your filter bubbles.)
- What apps or websites do you spend the most time in?
    - Why do you use them? For example, to keep in touch with friends, to learn about a specific topic, and so on.
    - If that particular app has sponsored content or ads or posts from people you don't follow, mixed in with content you follow, what do you notice about the suggestions presented to you?
- As an experiment, try a search in Google and then have a friend or family member do the same search. How do your results look the same? How do they differ?
- How might your views on a topic (social issue, current event, etc.) impact how you look for information and, in turn, your filter bubbles?

- As Christians, what might be some implications of living in
  filter bubbles in how we interact with others? For example:
  - Are you less likely to interact with people who have
    religious or political views different from your own?
  - Are you more likely to interact only with other Chris-
    tians or people you know?
  - How might your faith be informed by what you see
    within your bubbles?
- Think about one area of your online habits you might like
  to change—spending less time on your phone, engaging with
  different perspectives, reading more about the information
  landscape, and so on. What would it look like to ask someone
  to hold you accountable in doing so for a week or two? (See
  exercise 1.2 for specific steps.)

EXERCISE 1.1: FILTER BUBBLE

This chapter introduced the concept of the filter bubble and that
what we do online can limit or determine what we see based
on our past searching or browsing habits. Use these steps to notice and reflect on bubbles you might be experiencing in your
online spaces.

STEP 1. List the different apps you've used on your phone over
the last few days or week.

STEP 2. Think back over the ads you saw (sometimes labeled
"Sponsored") or the news that came up in your feeds. On some
platforms, you may see this content as frequently as every two
or three posts in your feed.

STEP 3. Make a list of the types of things you saw that were similar or repeating. For example, maybe you saw a lot of ads for
cleaning products or kitchenware or a number of news stories
on a similar topic.

STEP 4. What patterns or filter bubbles do you notice? Did you click on a particular news story or sponsored post and now are seeing those things show up in different apps or platforms? For example, did you click on a sponsored ad in Instagram, and now you also see similar ads in Facebook?

STEP 5. Reflect on your filter bubbles. What might they say about your information-seeking habits?

STEP 6. Consider asking a friend to do a similar or the same exercise, and compare notes. What do you notice about each other's filter bubbles? (Not in a judgmental way but a curious way.)

STEP 7. Reflect on this question: If you're honest, how might these filter bubbles or patterns impact the way you see the world, whether it's current events, a social issue, or even which products to buy?

EXERCISE 1.2: HABITS

This chapter also looked at the big picture of how information is structured. Just like it's helpful for us to regularly reflect on our day-to-day habits, part of being wise online includes regular reflection around our online habits. Use this exercise to reflect on how you might consider some changes in your own online habits. Of course, intentional growth takes commitment and time and probably more than just this one exercise. But hopefully reflecting on your habits will allow you to take a first step.

STEP 1. Reflect on your online habits by making a list of the things you want to change in your online interactions. For example, this could be anything from spending less time on your phone to less time in a specific app to reading a specified number of news sources. Or maybe you want to explore new apps or ways of getting information.

STEP 2. Look over your list. Which of those habits do you want to start by changing? Consider praying over your list and asking God whether he's prompting you to focus on a specific area.

STEP 3. Circle one habit you want to start with. Change is easier when we start with one step rather than tackle a whole list of new habits at once.

STEP 4. Write down two or three concrete steps you can take to change the habit. For example, if you want to spend less time in a specific app, set up a timer on your phone that kicks you out of the app after a certain number of minutes. Or you could keep your phone in a drawer when you work so you feel less likely to check it.

STEP 5. Make a plan for one or two weeks on how you'll take these steps. Will you do them all once? Or start with one, and add the others over the course of the two weeks? Again, smaller steps will help you be more successful. Changing everything at once could get overwhelming and result in no changes.

STEP 6. Think of one person who could hold you accountable. Text or call them and ask whether they'll check in on your progress.

STEP 7. At the end of the week or two weeks, journal or reflect or pray over what you noticed or learned about yourself and your online spaces. How will you maintain any changes you want to keep?

ADDITIONAL RESOURCES

Center for Humane Technology. https://www.humanetech.com/. This nonprofit organization is composed of many individuals who used to work for large technology and social media companies. They produced the documentary *The Social Dilemma* and are working to reimagine digital infrastructure. Their website provides many resources around their work, links to their podcast, and information about our current information landscape.

Kantayya, Shalini, dir. *Coded Bias*. 2020. Documentary available on Netflix. This documentary covers ways in which facial recognition and artificial intelligence algorithms demonstrate bias, particularly toward people of color.

Noble, Safiya Umoja. *Algorithms of Oppression: How Search Engines Reinforce Racism*. New York: New York University Press, 2018. This book discusses ways in which our current algorithms, particularly the ones used by big technology companies, are biased and oppress people of color.

O'Neil, Cathy. "The Era of Blind Faith in Big Data Must End." TED video. April 2017. https://www.ted.com/talks/cathy_o_neil_the _era_of_blind_faith_in_big_data_must_end?language=en. This TED talk is a great summary of a number of different and practical ways that algorithms can create injustice and unfair outcomes. O'Neil also wrote a book called *Weapons of Math Destruction* if you want to learn even more.

Orlowski, Jeff, dir. *The Social Dilemma*. 2020. Documentary available on Netflix. This documentary covers a lot of aspects of the information landscape, from algorithms to mental health concerns to misinformation.

Pariser, Eli. "Beware Online Filter Bubbles." TED video. March 2011. https://www.ted.com/talks/eli_pariser_beware_online_filter_bub bles?language=en. A great summary of his book; in this TED talk, Pariser lays out the basics of filter bubbles and how they impact what we see online. Like the book, it's a bit dated but still very relevant.

———. *The Filter Bubble: How the New Personalized Web Is Changing What We Read and How We Think*. New York: Penguin, 2011. Although this book was published over ten years ago (a long time in technology!), it is a good introduction to the concept of filter bubbles and how personalization affects our online spaces.

Project Information Literacy. Life in the Age of Algorithms, 2020. https://projectinfolit.org/pubs/algorithm-study/pil_algorithm -study_2020-01-15_algo-figure.png. This is the graphic associated with the study mentioned in this chapter. It's a clear and succinct summary of how the data collected about us online is fed into algorithms and can lead to division in our relationships.

CHAPTER 2

The Wide-Open
Information Landscape

In our conversations about faith and fake news, the primary thing we all need to understand about the online and information landscapes are the algorithms we talked about in chapter 1. I emphasize algorithms because they have the power to define so much of what we see online. In a world and culture that are driven by so many online spaces, we need to be aware of the algorithms that control those spaces in order to love our neighbors better and have productive and civil conversations with those around us—not necessarily conversations to change someone's mind but conversations that point to truth and to kindness.

However, I also think there are other pieces of the information landscape that are incredibly helpful to understand as we try to be thoughtful and wise in our online spaces: pieces like scholarly or scientific research, paywalls, and so on, which we'll cover in this chapter. These other aspects will give you a more comprehensive understanding of the online world and how it works. Some of you may be thinking, "What are these technical things doing in a book about faith?" I've had a similar response in live classes I've taught. I don't want to turn this into a textbook on the information landscape, but again, the more we can understand how information is structured, created, and organized, the more effective we'll be at navigating our online worlds.

In the past, I spent time studying missions, community development, and cross-cultural living and communication. In college, I studied abroad in Tanzania where I learned how to live in another culture. I took classes in culture, cross-cultural communication, and community development, which taught me to think about how to live effectively in another culture. While studying to get my master's in library science, I also focused on classes that centered on community development with regard to technology and libraries. And later, after I finished my master's degree, I spent 2011 and 2012 in Uganda as a missionary, where I worked as a librarian in a theological college setting. All of these classes and cross-cultural experiences taught me the importance of understanding a culture and the importance of being a learner before I tried to make changes. I was taught by other missionaries and community development workers to first look at my context and engage with the people around me before choosing how to move forward. This has impacted the way I look at the world over and over as I've entered new spaces and sought to first understand the context I move into before trying to make changes to it. When I don't do this, I find I'm more likely to judge the context in which I find myself—what's being done and the people who are part of it. Without this approach, I'm more likely to set myself up in some sort of us-versus-them mentality, seeing the new context as separate from me instead of a place I can engage with wholly.

Similarly, my current church in Minneapolis talks regularly about recognizing that God is already at work in the world—we don't bring God to new spaces but join in the work he's already doing in our schools, neighborhoods, workplaces, and so on. It's part of Mill City Church's DNA to ask questions about what God is already doing before starting something new, and that mentality has spilled into many areas of my life.

We can adopt a similar, cross-cultural mindset toward our online spaces. Learning how the information landscape works, how it's structured, and the things to watch out for will all help us engage more effectively and love our neighbors well. By learning about the culture first and acting second, we'll be more prepared to act carefully. We can also believe that God is already at work in these spaces, and by learning how the spaces work, we'll be better able to join him in his work. We meet God in his redemption work, even online. Yes, there are changes to be made in online spaces—both within ourselves and within the overall online structures. But we need to first situate ourselves in the space in order to move forward. As we look at a few technical pieces of the internet and social media, keep these questions in your mind and reflect on them:

- What does learning about these things tell me about my culture and what's going on around me?
- How might knowing these things change the way I interact with others and my online spaces? How might knowing these things impact my faith?
- How might my faith show up (or not) in these spaces?
- How does this help me understand the world around me?
- How do these online structures impact the way I want to engage with others in these spaces and, yes, even love others?

It can be hard to see connections between our online spaces, our culture, and our faith. But they're all connected. We're whole human beings that exist within this particular time and culture in history that I don't think we can ignore. We exist within our physical neighborhoods, homes, and workplaces, and we also exist within our online spaces as we use them. Keeping these things in mind and understanding our culture will help us engage better in all these areas. As you read the rest of this chapter, continue to think about the connections between our culture and your faith.

SOCIAL MEDIA, WEBSITES, AND A CONSTELLATION OF INFORMATION

Over the past twenty years as more and more information has been made available online, it's become harder and harder to distinguish between different types of information. I've seen this in my work as a librarian at a university, especially as college students have grown up with most of their information available online. As we access more content online, it becomes harder to distinguish where things come from or what makes one type of content different from another type. For college students, I've seen a continued shift toward greater and greater confusion around evaluating sources, as I've worked with them for almost fifteen years. Now, I don't want to disparage college students and young adults. I don't think it's their fault. Many young adults and teenagers have never been without the internet or a smartphone. Is it any wonder they have trouble knowing what scholarly sources are when they've only ever seen those things on a screen, the same way they see news articles and videos? The more information we have online, the more those sources lose their physical cues, which in the past helped us understand information. This issue isn't unique to college students; many of us struggle with the same thing.

Statistics show that from 2011 to 2021 there was an increase in the amount of data or information created, captured, copied, and consumed worldwide from five zettabytes to seventy-nine zettabytes.[1] This is a lot of information! One zettabyte is equal to a trillion gigabytes. If you think about the amount of data you can hold on your computer or phone or on a flash drive, it's only a drop in the bucket compared to the amount of data and information being created and consumed around the world. It's no wonder that we're overwhelmed and struggle to understand it all. When so much data and information are created, this complicates how we focus our time and can make it even more challenging to find authoritative and trustworthy information.

There are so many different types of information available online. You can think of these as sorts of subcultures or subtypes of information within this larger information landscape and culture. Each of these smaller subcultures or information types have specific characteristics in how they display and post information. For example, if you search for a current event on a news website, you'll likely find information that differs from what a search for a current event on Twitter or Instagram would yield. Each platform will have its own language in how it talks about the event. How people interact on the platform will be different, too, as each space has different expectations and a unique structure. There may even be different values behind what's posted. Even more confusingly, many news stories are just as likely to masquerade as opinion pieces or advertisements. It's helpful to think about these different types within a very big and complicated landscape so that as we move between them, we're better able to navigate each of them.

It's also easy for us to talk about the internet as though it contains one kind of information or as though it's a monolith of information. But the internet is a huge connection of many different networks, and within each network there are many different platforms and types of information—those subcultures of information. In the same way our cultures overlap in our physical spaces, these cultures of information overlap online as well. For example, a news platform may have a website where they post their articles (which may also be published in a print newspaper), and then they may post the headline and image with a link to the full article on a social media platform, such as Instagram. The social media post acts as a conduit to get readers to the full article. Additionally, these platforms always change and update the content they post and create. I often tell the college students I work with that it's very hard to go back and find the same article twice if you don't save it the first time.

Content is constantly being created, and as all these platforms are connected, the connections can change or be updated.

This can make navigating the internet confusing, as multiple things may be connected. Have you ever heard a friend or family member say, "I read this on Facebook"? It's possible that they had read someone else's individual post, but it's just as likely that someone had posted a link to an article and that's what your friend referred to. This is an example of how different platforms overlap and we can find information in multiple ways. These platforms are often connected seamlessly in ways that make it difficult to know when we've left one and moved on to another.

Here are a few other definitions that may be helpful for you as you think about how you navigate your online spaces:

- Websites: These are the backbone of the content we navigate online. Note that many other types of information exist on websites. For example, Twitter is technically a website, but we use it as a social media platform for posting and sharing information. On the other hand, news organizations have websites that are more static, where they post news articles for us to read or consume with less interaction.
- Applications: Often shortened and called apps, these are the programs you download to your smartphone. Some might be used without any social interaction, such as a personal fitness tracker or a game, while others may be used for connecting with others, such as TikTok or Instagram.
- Social media posts: Social media platforms are types of websites or applications that allow you to post content or connect with others' posts. Many websites use social media posts to share the content from their websites in a different venue. Some posts are static, while others are more dynamic, like videos. Examples of social media that involve posting include Instagram, TikTok, Twitter, and Facebook.

- Search engines: These are the specific websites you use to search for content. Examples are Google, Bing, and lesser-known DuckDuckGo.
- Browsers: These are the computer or phone applications you use to browse the internet. Examples include Safari, Chrome, and Firefox. This is where you go to specific websites.

Some of these definitions may be new to you, or they may be something you're very familiar with. Regardless, reflect for a minute on how many different places information lives—all these platforms and avenues for people to share their content, opinions, news, and more. Think about how much has changed in the last fifty years and how much information you have access to through these platforms. We have access to so much, and simply noticing that is important as we continue to move forward with practicing wisdom online.

PAYWALLS AND THE MYTH OF FREE INFORMATION

The next thing to understand in our information landscape is that not all information online is freely available. Some of you are thinking, "duh!" but some of you might not have thought about this before. Have you ever tried looking at an article, possibly from an online news source, and saw a message that said something like, "You have two free articles remaining"? Or maybe you weren't able to see an article at all but were instead asked to subscribe to the magazine or newspaper or at least create an account? This happened to me just the other day as I tried to navigate to a newspaper article. I was able to scroll to the second sentence, and then a pop-up covered my screen asking me to subscribe. These are examples of paywalls. Paywalls are ways to restrict access to certain materials without a subscription, and they apply to many kinds of platforms, most notably newspapers and magazines.

However, because so much information online *is* free, we can forget that not all of it is available without payment. We might also forget that free doesn't always mean best. Free information and news are easy to access, but that doesn't mean you get the most credible or unbiased information. And yet, because the paywalls slow us down, we don't always continue to pursue the information. How many times have you come across one of those paywalls and just switched to a different piece of content or a different article, skipping what you wanted to read originally?

But next time you go to a news website that doesn't require you to pay for a subscription, notice how many ads are on the site. It costs money to host information online—for computer servers and website designers and the internet and more. If it's a news site, they also need money to pay their reporters and journalists. Some platforms require a subscription to cover those costs. Other websites rely on advertisements from other companies. Many websites and platforms rely on a mix of both. To some extent, the ways these websites track our interactions with their content is also part of the payment we give them. I use an ad blocker on my internet browser and have found many times I've tried going to certain news sites and been met with a message that essentially says, "We see you're using an ad blocker. Turn it off to see our content or sign up for an account." Basically, those sites say that they get revenue via the ads on their website, and an ad blocker won't allow us to see those ads, meaning they won't get the same revenue.

Historically, people primarily bought information by buying newspapers and books. It wasn't always free a hundred years ago either. But somehow because a lot of information *is* free online, many people assume it's all free, or that it all should be free.

This is such an important thing to realize when it comes to navigating our online spaces. If we rely solely on the information we can access freely, we miss a lot of information! It's very easy for people to create websites and social media accounts as long as they have an internet connection. It's also easy to make those sites look convincing and for them to become platforms for misinformation and disinformation. There are so many places to go for information, and it's important for us to know how to access different kinds of information as opposed to only relying on what's freely available.

So how do you get around those paywalls? You have a few options. First, if it's a news site that you frequent and it's trustworthy, consider subscribing directly. Support good journalism by paying for access. You'll be better informed because of it. Last year I found there were several prominent, national newspapers that I regularly accessed but was able to see only a few articles per month, so I decided to subscribe so that I'd have consistent access. It was a sacrifice for my budget but worth the cost in order to support the quality information, regularly see the content, and be well informed.

Second, consider checking with several local libraries for access to content. For example, your local public library will often provide access to online newspapers and magazines. Whether it's general, online news access or specific articles, your local public library can often provide access for you. It may be online or in person, but it's worth checking since that's your taxpayer dollars at work. Additionally, if you live near any publicly funded colleges or universities, they may be able to provide you with limited guest access to some resources, such as newspapers or scholarly journals. When I worked at a local community college in the past, we were obligated to provide limited access to community members because we were a locally funded college. Many state universities have similar policies, although you may be limited on how long you can use their resources. It'll take a bit more initiative on your part, but it's worth seeing whether there are ways to get access to information behind paywalls so that you can be well informed and access a wider variety of resources.

Remember if you rely only on what's free—while not all bad information—you'll be limiting what you can access and consume. And to be honest, some of that free information really isn't all that great. If we want to be truth-seekers, we may need to put in some effort in order to actually find and access that truth.

Please know, too, that many scholars and activists work to create more open access information—quality information that's freely available. These open access principles encourage researchers and others to share their findings openly, without barriers. You may even see content online listed as "open access." This is an exciting and important movement in our online spaces, but it's not everywhere, and not everything falls under this type of information. So, in the meantime, we may need to find alternative ways to access information, news, and other resources.

As you think about paywalls and free information, reflect for a minute on where you get your information from. Do you rely only on the information and news you can get for free? Why or why not? Or are you willing to invest in quality information, if necessary? Not all information is created equal, and not all free information is quality. I'm not suggesting that you purchase a subscription to a highly biased or controversial news site (we'll learn more later how you can determine whether a news site is credible), but if we want to be truth-seekers, it's helpful to think about *all* the places we may need to look to find that truth and be willing to seek them out.

NAVIGATING RESEARCH, SCHOLARLY INFORMATION, AND THE SCIENTIFIC PROCESS

The current (as of this writing) COVID-19 pandemic has highlighted another area that's often misunderstood when navigating online spaces: scholarly research. Throughout the pandemic, news sites, social media, and radio sound bites have mentioned "new studies" and what was found about various aspects of the coronavirus, from masking to vaccines to symptoms to long-term effects. It's not unusual to hear public officials or newscasters share results of "a recent study." This has created a lot of confusion, especially in the United States, throughout the pandemic, as sometimes those studies have seemingly contradicted each other.

This can also be confusing because those recent studies are examples of scholarly research studies, which are often behind those paywalls we just discussed. They're published in scholarly journals, which usually require a subscription to access. The studies are usually not available online for free, and depending on where the information comes from, you may have access only to an abstract, or summary, of the research article. Many people read the abstract and think that they understand the research. Or they get frustrated that they can't read the entire article and turn to free sources of information instead.

The reality is that those scholarly research articles are incredibly important to understanding the nuances of current issues and especially science and health issues. They're in-depth research studies conducted by people who are experts in their fields: psychologists, biologists, infectious disease experts, sociologists, and so on. The research is then often reviewed for accuracy by other experts in the field (those articles are called peer-reviewed). These research articles form the backbone of many of our academic fields, and if we don't understand the basics of how research works, where it's published, and how to access it, we might mistake that free information we found online for being good-enough information or the whole story of the research.

Importantly, scholarly information is most often written for other experts or scholars in the field, not for the average lay person like you or me (unless, of course, you're an expert in a particular field!). These scholars in essence have a type of long conversation about their fields that they've spent years studying. As one researcher writes a scholarly article, others read it, use it in their own research, and cite it. Although we may have access to some of their research or may read some of the articles' abstracts, it can be helpful to remember that we may see only a very small piece of that entire conversation. These articles have often been building on each other for years. And if we haven't spent much time studying the field, our understanding may be even more limited.

Finally, it's also worth noting that a lot of scholarly research follows the scientific process. Remember learning about the scientific process in elementary or middle school? We learned to come up with a hypothesis, test it, and then build on our results. See the image below for an example of the simplified scientific method. Notice that the conclusions lead right back into a question and start the cycle all over again.

In the last few years, I've sometimes wondered whether we've forgotten how the scientific process works. As scientists and scholars write about their research, more scholars read the articles, try to replicate the research, or build on it. In library jargon, we sometimes call this the "scholarly conversation." This conversation happens among scholars and scientists through their research and is part of why it can feel like the science around different topics changes.

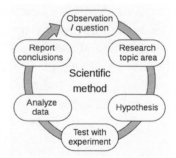

The scientific method, a representation of the scientific process, showing the cyclical nature of research.

We've seen this throughout the COVID-19 pandemic: Scientists make a claim, and then later the claims shift or are changed by the same or additional experts. This is part of the other reason scholarly research can be so confusing to many of us. But in reality, this change in the research is okay and normal. We want our scientists to keep making new discoveries about the world.

Unfortunately, this has led to a spirit of distrust. I suspect some people—maybe even you—think, "Whom can I trust if things keep changing?"

But in order to seek the truth about a situation, we need to understand this process. Instead of being quite so skeptical of the scientists and researchers, we also need to be okay with the changes we see so that we can better understand complex issues. In a very basic sense, if science didn't advance and change, we'd still believe the earth is flat. Instead, as people of faith, we have an opportunity to see God at work in the nuances and research of science and other scholarly information. As the creator of the world, he's the ultimate scientist. What would it look like for us to embrace the scientific process as part of our faith and to trust that he's the one who ultimately gives scientists their wisdom? And what would it look like to believe that science is God-inspired, revealed by him? Yes, we should hold people accountable, and there's a place for skepticism. But it's also easy to go down a rabbit trail of assuming everything is untrustworthy, and we have an opportunity to also find a place in our faith for scientific expertise and vice versa.

THE MYTH OF DOING YOUR OWN RESEARCH

Along with not always understanding how scientific research works and with the increase of information available online, I've also noticed an increase in the last few years—especially in the midst of a global pandemic—of people saying or posting that they did their own research and choose to do X, Y, or Z because of what they found. I've noticed this comment mostly around health information but other things as well.

Maybe you've found yourself doing the same thing. Do you have topics or issues that you prefer to research for yourself? As a librarian, I'm obviously a huge fan of people researching and exploring information. But where this can get tricky is if we equate our own research with being an expert on a particular subject. For example, in 2021 when I found out I was pregnant, I had to be careful not to overresearch every pain I felt or question I had and remind myself to wait for appointments with my health-care provider to ask questions. It's not that my using Google to research my pregnancy symptoms was all bad; it's that just because I had access to so much information didn't mean I always knew how to interpret it or whether it was all correct. I needed to also rely on my health-care providers, who have studied pregnancy for years, to answer my questions. We'll talk more about knowing whether someone is an expert in chapter 4, but the idea of doing your own research is a double-edged sword if we're not careful, and one we need to be aware of in online spaces.

Maybe you've even seen those gift mugs available online about not mistaking a Google search with a specific degree—mugs that say, "Please don't mistake your Google search for my MD," or "Please don't mistake your Google search for my law degree." I've seen these for a variety of professions, from medical doctors to lawyers to librarians. And while these mugs are a bit tongue-in-cheek and funny, there's some truth to them. Our ability to google almost anything should be taken with a grain of salt. We aren't experts on all the things we google or find online. Yes, we'll find good information on most topics, but remember those algorithms? Depending on what we've searched before, we may end up in a loop of misinformation or at the least not great information. Another way of saying this might be to ask, "Do you want to use the same tool you use to find restaurant reviews for researching your medical concern?"

Here's another example. How many times during the COVID-19 pandemic have you heard someone say, "Well, I researched this and I'm going to do . . . ," referring to anything from wearing a mask to not wearing a mask, getting a vaccine to not getting one, and so on. I've had multiple people tell me that they did their own research on the pandemic and masks and believe that masks don't work. On the other hand, the public health community has said over and over that wearing masks can help slow the spread of the COVID-19 pandemic (admittedly after some initial, confusing comments that masks weren't the answer). These types of comments from people in my life who claim to have done their own research make me wonder *where* they research to come to this conclusion when so much of the medical and health communities say the opposite. Again, I don't mean to make this political—how a health crisis became political is a whole different story—but it's a good example of how while we have access to so much information about a topic (COVID-19) and to so many voices commentating on the issue, it may be harder for us to interpret and do our own research than we realize.

People spend hours digging around online and believe they've solved a problem or found something the experts have missed. We'll see more, in a later chapter, about how to tell whether someone is an expert, but for now, it's worth thinking about the areas in which we tend to research for ourselves with or without looking to experts for their expertise. Yes, we have tools to do our own research—and we should—but it's also important to know where our own knowledge ends and where our ability to interpret what we find may be limited.

Even in our faith communities we do this, right? We hire pastors who have studied theology and the Bible to lead our churches. Our youth and children's ministries are run by people who have studied and practiced those specific types of ministries. In our personal lives, we visit therapists when we need mental health help. Yes, we can find lots of information online on many topics, but we need to know when to seek the experts. Reflect on the ways in which you've chosen experts to follow—or not—and why you chose those particular experts.

This is an area where we can find a bit more nuance. We can both use our own wisdom and research and understanding of the world *and* trust experts. We can choose to say that their research is enough for us. We can choose to research a topic, know our limits, and get to a point where we can say that the experts know more than we do.

THIS INFORMATION LANDSCAPE AND OUR FAITH

Although this chapter covers a lot of specific aspects of the information landscape, in our current climate of distrust and divisiveness, they're worth understanding. The more we can understand our information culture, the more effective we can be in engaging with information and others. I often think about how Jesus navigated his world, traveling to different parts of the region, interacting with people from different towns and areas. His way of interacting with people wasn't always the same. Sometimes he told parables, sometimes he healed people, other times he went to be alone, and other times he was simply in company with his disciples. Jesus didn't inhabit his spaces the same all the time, and there's an invitation for us to think about the different spaces we inhabit and how we want to engage more intentionally. Although we live hundreds of years later, I wonder what it would look like for us to observe the different spaces we inhabit—both online spaces and physical spaces—and be willing to see them for what they are. How does understanding these spaces help us decide how to move forward?

REFLECTION QUESTIONS

- Which of these concepts in this chapter was or is new to you?
- How might learning more about the online spaces in our culture impact the way you want to interact online? How does understanding these things help you understand the world better?
- As a Christian, how does learning about these different things affect the way you might want to behave or interact online?

What does learning about these things tell you about your culture and what's going on around you?

- How might knowing these things about the information landscape change the way you interact with others in your online spaces? How might knowing these things impact your faith?
- How do these online structures impact the way you want to engage with others in these spaces and, yes, even love others?
- What's something you tried to research on your own but later realized you needed the help of experts to understand the concept?
- Which of these different information subcultures are you most comfortable navigating? Social media? News websites? Blogs? Why do you think that is?

EXERCISE 2: TYPES OF INFORMATION

This chapter contained different examples of the types of platforms and information that make up our online landscape and culture and, in turn, impact our culture at large. It can be helpful to also recognize the differences between different types of information in order to better know what you're looking at and how to engage with it. This exercise will walk you through some of the different types or subcultures of information and reflect on how they're the same and how they're different.

STEP 1. Think of a topic or current event that you've seen covered in a lot of different platforms. You'll try searching for this topic in a few different places.

STEP 2. Try searching that issue, event, or topic in Google Scholar (scholar.google.com). This platform will give you scholarly research from across the internet—scholarly research articles, book chapters, and so on. Click on a few of the results. What do you notice about the type of language used? What do you notice about the type of information you find?

STEP 3. Go to the Associated Press website (apnews.com)—a well-known news agency. Try searching for your topic or event again. What do you notice about how the information is portrayed by the news? How does it compare to what you saw in Google Scholar?

STEP 4. Finally, pick a social media platform, such as Twitter, Instagram, or Facebook, and search your topic or event one more time. What do you notice this time about what you find? What type of language is used? Who is posting?

STEP 5. Think about all three of your searches. How are they similar? How are they different? Reflect on how you might engage differently depending on which platform you use or what type of information you look at. How can paying attention to your own way of interacting impact the way you engage online?

ADDITIONAL RESOURCES

DuckDuckGo. https://duckduckgo.com. This search engine is an alternative to using Google for finding information online. Many people like using DuckDuckGo because there's less personalization and tracking. They find this freeing, as it removes them from some of the filter bubbles they've found themselves in. Note that your search results will look and be different from those of a Google search, but many find this a helpful thing.

Goel, Vinod. "Vaccine Hesitancy: Why 'Doing Your Own Research' Doesn't Work, but Reason Alone Won't Change Minds." The Conversation. February 17, 2022. https://theconversation.com /vaccine-hesitancy-why-doing-your-own-research-doesnt-work -but-reason-alone-wont-change-minds-169814. This short article written by a neuroscientist reminds us that sometimes we can't do our own research and that relying on specialists can help us make better decisions. He also points out the role that other parts of our brains take in making decisions. We aren't all rational all the time, which can also affect our ability to do our own research.

"How to Find Health Information You Can Trust (with Dr. Jen Gunter)." In *How to Be a Better Human*. Podcast audio. November 8, 2021. https://open.spotify.com/episode/5notokq76n WQWACXFdfYr2?si=d8_TaozYQP-BkN3PEUyVKA. While this episode focuses primarily on health information and misinformation, there are many helpful tips for finding reliable information online. It also includes reminders that not all information you find online is created equal. Some of the tips Dr. Gunter shares are similar to the ones you'll read about in chapter 4.

Teaching and Learning, University Libraries. "A Source's Neighborhood." In *Choosing and Using Sources: A Guide to Academic Research*. The Ohio State University. https://ohiostate.pressbooks .pub/choosingsources/chapter/a-sources-neighborhood/. This ebook is written primarily for college students, but this particular chapter is helpful in encouraging us to think about how the information we seek fits into the larger information landscape. They use the term "neighborhood" to help us think about how web content fits in relation to the things around it.

CHAPTER 3

A World of Fake News

What would a book on faith and fake news be without a chapter directly addressing fake news? It's a loaded term, to be sure. As we saw in the introduction, misinformation and disinformation aren't the same thing, but the terms get used interchangeably. "Fake news" is another term that gets tossed in the mix of confusing language about information. So, as we finish up our conversation in this section about the information landscape as a whole, it's worth mentioning a few things about fake news specifically.

Fake news, like its cousins misinformation and disinformation, isn't a new phenomenon. There are a lot of different definitions of "fake news," but generally it's a broad term and means news that's misleading or false. It's specifically about news, whereas the terms "misinformation" and "disinformation" may be more focused on information in general. Additionally, like other forms of false information, the way fake news spreads now—through social media and the internet—has changed significantly in the last thirty years. People have always spread false stories about news, events, and people. That isn't new, and similarly to our current information landscape, some of the spreading of false information was intentional, and some of it happened through sharing and resharing information that turned into a game of telephone. As always, it's worth pointing out that the term "fake news" shouldn't be used to refer to news someone just disagrees with. Fake doesn't mean anything that doesn't conform to our viewpoints.

In the fall of 2021, I was interviewed for a podcast episode called "Where the Gospel Meets Fake News," by the *Love Thy Neighborhood* podcast, in partnership with the *Holy Post* podcast. In this episode, they outlined a number of things relating to fake news and how it impacts our witness as Christians. They specifically called out how, as Christians, we can't be a part of spreading lies, misinformation, and deception. That isn't who Jesus was or is and not what he would want from us.

Being a guest on this podcast meant I was interviewed about my perspective but didn't quite know how my interview would fit into the entire episode until the podcast was released. I was told they were interviewing several people, and I was specifically interviewed about my classes and how I've been encouraging churches to address misinformation. But I didn't know what else they had planned. When the episode was released and I heard the whole thing, I was blown away by a story the hosts told in the beginning of the episode: Matthew 28:11–15. Here in the gospel is an example of fake news, or false information, spreading from the very beginning of Christianity. After Jesus is resurrected, the guards from the tomb tell the priests what happened, and the priests specifically tell the guards to lie and say that the disciples stole Jesus's body. Even for the church, false information isn't new.

In case you need a reminder, here's the passage from Matthew 28, which takes place right after Jesus appears to Mary Magdalene and Mary:

> ¹¹While the women were on their way, some of the guards went into the city and reported to the chief priests everything

that had happened. [12]When the chief priests had met with the elders and devised a plan, they gave the soldiers a large sum of money, [13]telling them, "You are to say, 'His disciples came during the night and stole him away while we were asleep.' [14]If this report gets to the governor, we will satisfy him and keep you out of trouble." [15]So the soldiers took the money and did as they were instructed. And this story has been widely circulated among the Jews to this very day. (NLT)

I had heard this story before as part of the Easter story but hadn't put it in the context of false news. I've been thinking about it since that podcast came out, thinking about how at the very beginning of Christianity, people told false information about Jesus. Fake news isn't new, and this story demonstrates the lengths people will go to in order to keep some things hidden. This has happened throughout history and even as part of our own faith tradition.

Fast forward a few hundred years, and in her book *True or False: A CIA Analyst's Guide to Spotting Fake News* Cindy Otis gives many examples of fake news and misinformation throughout history. Interestingly, throughout history, changes in technology have played a role in the spread of fake news. When the printing press was invented and literacy rates increased, it became even easier for people to create and pass along fake information in the form of pamphlets and posters. Newspapers in early American history were responsible for spreading misinformation and disinformation. Years later, there are examples of stories on the radio in the early twentieth century contributing to the spread of misinformation. As technologies changed throughout history, there's an increase in the spread of false information. Is it any wonder that with our huge increase of information online, there's also an increase in misinformation?

As I've mentioned already in earlier chapters, the more we understand about the information landscape (and the history of it), the more we can engage wisely and effectively with news, social media, and other online platforms. Recognizing that false information, or fake news, has always been an issue can take out some of the fear or urgency of what we see in our current culture. Many of us want to make things better *right now*. We see how our world is full of misinformation and get overwhelmed and want to address it all. We want our family to stop believing a conspiracy theory today. It's a noble cause and one I'm obviously passionate about. But when I think about how misinformation has always been a part of humanity, I'm able to take a step back. Yes, we can and should still address it, but maybe we don't have to feel quite so desperate to fix it immediately. So many efforts to make changes in our world are long games; social changes rarely happen overnight. Keeping a long game frame of reference can help us be more intentional in these spaces without feeling frantic about it.

As people of faith, we can also use this space to discern where and with whom the Holy Spirit might be calling us to engage. There are many areas in which false information shows up in our online spaces. What might be your role in addressing it? Some of us will feel called to change the way we look at information, others of us will be called to address it with those in our lives more directly. I never want to discount the ways in which God might ask us to each engage with this differently.

We also need to think about how loaded the term "fake news" is and be judicious about how or where we use it. If we want to be salt and light in our world, it would be helpful for us to also be careful about the words we use. Throwing around loaded terms like "fake news" isn't helpful as we try to discern truth and love the people around us or speak truth to them. I've heard stories over and over of people being blamed for sharing fake news, which inevitably shuts them down or only makes them feel defensive. We have an opportunity to use words wisely, and it starts by not carelessly using terms that are so controversial, particularly if they're pointed at others.

Another thing that may seem obvious but is important to mention directly is that "fake news" doesn't mean news that you disagree with. It can be hard to engage with information we disagree with—that's human nature—but that doesn't make it fake or incorrect or false. We'll continue talking about this later, but it's important we're as curious as possible—meaning we don't want to automatically label something "fake" just because we're unsure whether it's true or because we disagree with it or because we have an emotional reaction to it. Unfortunately, the term "fake news" is often used by politicians and others to mean "information I don't like or disagree with" or casually tossed around in emotional contexts. Throughout this book, I tend to use the terms "misinformation" and "disinformation" or "false information" because the term "fake news" can be so loaded.

Another term that's closely aligned with "fake news" is "conspiracy theory." This is another term that makes people squirm and elicits strong reactions. Conspiracy theories, like fake news (or just purposely false information) aren't new. Again, the way these theories spread has changed significantly in recent years as the internet and social media have increased the amount of information available to us. But the idea that people spread conspiracy theories isn't new to the internet.

Conspiracy theories, in contrast to general misinformation, involve a belief that someone else or another organization or group is responsible for an event or for something going on in our world. We often hear them connected to government(s) or other large organizations. Conspiracy theories tend to be a bit darker than just misinformation, because they usually involve a belief that someone, or a group of people in the case of an organization, is behind what's causing a problem.

Recently in a workshop with a church, someone brought up a conspiracy theory, although I don't think they'd have labeled it that. I asked what type of techniques the participants already used to determine whether something online was true. Someone said, "If I see content get removed from Facebook, like when a video or article is no longer available, I know it [the removed content] must be true because they don't want me to see it." There's a lot to unpack here, but to me, this is an example of the type of distrust that helps conspiracy theories continue to circulate. The person that made this comment was well intentioned in sharing their ideas about how they evaluate information. But they were, from my perspective, also incredibly distrustful of the online environment. Without saying it, they also implied that the social media companies or websites censored the information that needed to be made public.

Although, at the moment, I was unable to fully address the comment, my first question would have been "Who is 'they'? *Who* doesn't want you to see information?" The very nature of labeling something as being the fault of someone else made me think of conspiracy theories, since they're specifically focused on a larger organization or government being responsible for some sort of thing happening. I got the sense that this particular person was also concerned about censorship and their first amendment rights. It's possible that there was also a conflict between what they saw online—or how they saw information removed—and their own personal values.

Many of us have seen this type of removal of information happen on YouTube, Facebook, and other platforms. Sometimes the content is grayed out and covered over with a message saying it's been removed. Other times there's just a notice below the content saying it's been checked by independent fact-checkers and may be outdated or may not be correct. Either way, the message probably says something along the lines of "this information has been checked and may contain false or outdated information." We've seen an increase in these posts throughout the pandemic.

Those of us who live in the United States do have the right to free speech under the First Amendment. However, censorship and our First Amendment rights to free speech in the United States aren't the same as social media companies (YouTube, Facebook, Instagram, etc.) taking down misinformation from their platforms. When we agree to use social media, we agree to their terms or their use policies. These platforms are private companies that have their own policies around information and misinformation and, as such, can remove or flag content according to their policies. Remember that by agreeing to use social media and other platforms, you agree to *their* terms of service. Remember those algorithms collect our data in return for our free use of the platforms. You can also look up many of their misinformation policies on their websites if you're unsure of what might be included. Our first amendment right to free speech protects us from the *government* limiting our rights, not private companies.

Finally, there's false information and fake news easily available online. We find it on social media; we find it elsewhere. You've probably come across fake news, whether you realized it or not. Not all information is created equal, and it's important to call out misinformation for what it is: false information. As Christians, we need to be aware of what happens in our online spaces and on our social media feeds in order to be part of the solution. The next section of the book will give you some tools to find and call out misinformation, but it's worth overstating that there are gradients of information. Some are more credible and trustworthy than others. The more we can acknowledge our current reality, the more prepared we'll be to combat it.

Satan must love this web of false information and the literal fake news we see online. He's the father of lies. Fake news and false information are right up his alley. Let's use our identity as people of the truth to be part of spreading truth and shutting down false information.

REFLECTION QUESTIONS

- Have you ever labeled something fake news out of frustration? Was it actually fake news or just something you disagreed with? How did you determine whether it was false?

- Think about how fake news and misinformation aren't new in the sense that they've always existed. Does that change your view of what's going on currently in our culture? If so, how? If not, why not?
- Have you ever been sucked into a conspiracy theory or fake news? How did you find out it was false information? Did you struggle to accept that you were wrong?
- Can you think of any specific conspiracy theories and identify the values or motivations behind why others might perceive it as truth? You can use the resources list for this chapter to find additional conspiracy theories if you're not sure of any specific ones.

EXERCISE 3: FAKE NEWS

This chapter summarized a number of things relating specifically to the concept of fake news or false information. The term "fake news" has become highly emotional in our culture and can create barriers for how we interact with information. Use this exercise to reflect on the ways you've seen fake news or false information impact yourself or those around you.

STEP 1. Think about the times you've heard the term "fake news" in conversation or through various media outlets. Did someone casually use the term? What did the term refer to?

STEP 2. The term "fake news" is incredibly loaded and controversial. When you heard the term, how did you respond, either internally or externally? Were you defensive? Did you agree with how the term was used?

STEP 3. Reflect on the ways in which you want to be part of fighting fake news and misinformation as a Christian. How does your faith impact the way you want to respond to fake news?

ADDITIONAL RESOURCES

Isaac, Joseph. "Why People Fall for Misinformation." TED video. September 2020. https://www.ted.com/talks/joseph_isaac_why_peo ple_fall_for_misinformation. This short video discusses a specific example of misinformation being spread for decades and why it's easy for us to buy into false information.

Levitin, Daniel. "Four Tricky Ways That Fake News Can Fool You." Ideas.ted.com. December 13, 2016. https://ideas.ted.com/four -tricky-ways-that-fake-news-can-fool-you/. This short article includes a few practical tips to help you identify information that may be false.

"List of Conspiracy Theories." Wikipedia. https://en.wikipedia.org /wiki/List_of_conspiracy_theories. Although by no means comprehensive, this list of conspiracy theories on Wikipedia is another place you can see a wide variety of these theories.

Otis, Cindy L. *True or False: A CIA Analyst's Guide to Spotting Fake News.* New York: Feiwel and Friends, 2020. This book gives a historical view of fake news throughout history, which is helpful for understanding the context in which we find ourselves. It also contains specific tools you can use to spot misinformation.

Posetti, Julie, and Alice Matthews. "A Short Guide to History of 'Fake News' and Disinformation." International Center for Journalists (ICFJ). July 2018. https://www.icfj.org/sites/default/files/2018 -07/A%20Short%20Guide%20to%20History%20of%20Fake%20 News%20and%20Disinformation_ICFJ%20Final.pdf. This document was created as part of a learning module for journalists but contains a helpful timeline of disinformation, dating back to before the invention of the printing press. Reflecting on how far back disinformation has been a problem can be helpful for us. Fake news can feel very urgent and dramatic, but it can be helpful to remind ourselves these aren't new things.

"Where the Gospel Meets Fake News." In *Love Thy Neighborhood.* Podcast audio. November 23, 2021. https://lovethyneighborhood

.org/episode-50-where-the-gospel-meets-fake-news/. This podcast, created in partnership with the *Holy Post* podcast, discusses a variety of aspects of fake news and how it impacts Christianity. Hosts Jesse Eubanks and Skye Jethani cover the history of false information as well as the current information climate that allows fake news to proliferate. Most importantly, they discuss the impact it has for Christians and the importance of *not* spreading misinformation. I share in this episode about the classes I offer churches, but there are a lot of additional takeaways in the episode about how our faith and fake news aren't compatible.

PART TWO

Evaluating Information

It's worth a pause here to see where we are before moving forward. As we saw earlier, these are steps to follow in order for us to be wise in our online spaces:

1. Understand the information landscape.
2. Evaluate the information you find, see, read, or hear.
3. Choose and discern how you want to engage with the information, including:
   a. loving your (online) neighbors and speaking truth to other people and those who believe misinformation;
   b. practicing humility in learning new perspectives.

In the first three chapters, we talked about different ways to understand the information landscape. Hopefully, reading a bit more about algorithms, paywalls, scholarly information, and so on gives you a better framework for the world and culture we live in and gives you space to reflect on your place as a Christian within that world. Hopefully, it allows you to place yourself within our current, online culture. And hopefully, if you were unfamiliar with some of these concepts, learning more about the online environment and landscape makes it a little less scary. It can be hard and overwhelming to engage with new things, so I always start with the big picture, giving people a chance to learn more about our current landscape and ensuring we're all on the same page before we move on to the next step.

Admittedly, some of the information around that information landscape can be a bit scary. Seeing how algorithms impact us and how conspiracy theories spread is uncomfortable. It could be easy to villainize all big technology companies and technology in general. But instead, we need to acknowledge where we are, understanding the larger picture, so we can move forward in doing our part to address misinformation. This next section will give you some specific tools and practices you can use to be part of making changes. We'll cover these tools in the next two chapters, and they'll give you some specific things you can try when you're online and wondering, "Is this true?"

Again, spreading misinformation isn't in our best interest as Christians, and learning some specific tools to use can help ensure we're not part of the misinformation and division problems so prevalent in our culture. We'll get to this in section 3, but there are different outcomes of using these tools, which may be helpful to have in your mind as you learn these practices. You may have the opportunity to practice humility and learn something new about a topic as you find out more information and the truth. Or you may have the opportunity to practice kindness and use what you learn to speak to others about misinformation. For now, we'll practice some techniques, but it will be helpful to think about that bigger picture as you learn them.

CHAPTER 4

Noticing Our Emotions

Now that we've discussed the information landscape in the first few chapters and spent time understanding how our culture is situated in and affected by online spaces, we can talk more about how to evaluate what you read, see, hear, and so on. Remember this is the second step in being a wise consumer of information: having some tools in your pocket that will help you fact-check or verify the information you engage with. This doesn't mean we have to fact-check everything or stop every time we read or watch the news, but having a few tools that allow you to better assess or evaluate will help you engage more thoughtfully with information.

But before we dive into some practical, fact-checking tools, we need to start with ourselves. In all my in-person classes on faith and fake news, I spend at least one session talking about our emotions in online spaces, which is what we'll discuss in this chapter. Before we look at practical tools of determining whether something is true, we need to build a habit of checking in with or examining our emotions. Our emotions are a helpful barometer as we lean into examining information online. While the practical, logical tools we'll examine in the next chapter are incredibly important, they don't exist in a vacuum. We aren't always rational, logical beings. We're complex humans with thoughts, emotions, and souls, and simply providing people with step-by-step tools isn't enough. This chapter on emotions helps us look more holistically at how we respond to our online environment.

Our emotions can also be a way for us to act differently in our online spaces. Someone recently said to me, "it seems like we all respond with our thumbs instead of our hearts when we're interacting with other people online," and I couldn't agree more. We often respond hastily, without taking stock of how our emotions might impact the way we interact with information or other people. As Christians, noticing more nuances in ourselves and our emotional state can help us behave differently in our online spaces. Our emotions are often information for us about our internal state, and paying attention to them provides us with additional data points for ourselves.

So first we need to pay attention to ourselves and our own emotions. In a recent class, I asked the participants to reflect for a minute on the emotions they often feel when they scroll through the news or social media. One gentleman raised his hand and said, "Anger. I feel angry when I read the news." I was grateful he was willing to admit that to a room of about twenty-five people, because a lot of the other participants resonated with him. This sparked a conversation around our emotional state online, which is the starting point for any kind of fact-checking or information evaluation. Before we can determine whether something is true, we need to pause and examine our internal responses. Our emotional state and internal responses can color the way we see information and impact the way we respond.

In fact, there are many studies that show that emotional content in online spaces spreads faster as it catches consumers' attention. For example, a study in 2014 showed that "anger is the emotion that travels fastest and farthest on social media, compared to all other emotions. As a result, those who post angry messages will inevitably have the greatest influence, and social media platforms will tend to be dominated by anger."[1] So, the gentleman in my workshop wasn't alone in his feelings of anger online. Anecdotally, others in the class agreed with him, and studies like this one also confirm the same thing. It's no surprise that if angry messages spread the fastest, many of us would feel angry when engaging with content online.

So, what does this have to do with fact-checking and evaluating information? Before we can dive into using specific tools and techniques in the next chapter, the first tool is actually a practice that starts with ourselves. As we saw in the first section of this book, websites and social media vie for our attention. These platforms want to keep us engaged on their site so they can make money. And in order to do that, a lot of content thrives on emotions. Think about the last time you scrolled through or watched the news. Which were the headlines that sparked your interest? Or the ones that caught your attention? Likely, they were the ones that elicited some sort of emotional response: anger, annoyance, disbelief, excitement.

Before we can even start to fact-check or verify a story or image, we need to pause and notice our emotions. That's not to say we don't have emotions or should ignore them, but we need to notice how our emotional reactions might impact our response in our online spaces. This can be difficult for many of us if we're not used to paying attention to our emotional state. It can be easy to go through life on autopilot, feeling our emotions but not really acknowledging them, or dwelling in them, unsure how to move past them. A therapist once told me that emotions are normal, natural, and neutral, meaning that we all have them (whether we pay attention or not!) and that they aren't good or bad. But he also encouraged me to pay attention to them, as they're a helpful barometer of our internal state.

In the church and in Christian circles, we often focus on the spiritual side of our world, emphasizing our prayer life or Bible-reading habits. In our school or work worlds, we can spend a lot of time focused on the logical side of our brains, primarily paying attention to checklists and logical next steps. In both cases, we can forget to pay attention to our emotional state. And because both misinformation and disinformation thrive on emotions, this is one area that we may need to grow in, in order to be wise and intentional online.

Four Moves and a Habit, a fact-checking framework developed by Mike Caulfield and explained in his ebook, *Web Literacy for Student Fact-Checkers*, includes various moves or fact-checking techniques, which we'll get to in the next chapter. But it also includes this important habit for us to adopt in order to navigate our online spaces more productively. The four moves refer to specific steps you can take in order to fact-check what you find online, while the habit Caulfield refers to is the process of noticing your emotions. This seems like an important step for us as Christians as we think about the passages that talk about being slow to anger or not letting the sun go down when we're angry:

- Proverbs 14:29: "Whoever is slow to anger has great understanding, but he who has a hasty temper exalts folly" (ESV).
- Ephesians 4:26: "'In your anger do not sin': Do not let the sun go down while you are still angry" (NIV).

These are words and advice many of us have heard if we've grown up in a Christian faith tradition—good advice not only for our day-to-day relationships but also for our online spaces. After talking in the workshop about content that made people angry, I spent a lot of time thinking about how our internal state plays such a big role in how we respond to others. Later that week, I was exploring a Bible app called Dwell, which allows the user to listen to the Bible in different translations and voices. I found a playlist of Bible passages called "I feel angry" and decided to listen to it, since I had just been talking about this concept in the class. The first passage was from James 1:19–20:

> [19]My dear brothers and sisters, take note of this: Everyone should be quick to listen, slow to speak and slow to become angry, [20]because human anger does not produce the righteousness that God desires. (NIV)

This jumped out at me as such a good principle for our online spaces and relationships in addition to the other passages I listed earlier. I shared it with those in my workshop the next week, and it sparked some additional conversation about how, yes, we experience anger in our world, but we can choose how we'll respond to it. Caulfield puts it this way in his ebook:

> Our normal inclination is to ignore verification needs when we react strongly to content, and researchers have found that content that causes strong emotions (both positive and negative) spreads the fastest through our social networks. Savvy activists and advocates take advantage of this flaw of ours, getting past our filters by posting material that goes straight to our hearts. . . . Use your emotions as a reminder. Strong emotions should become a trigger for your new fact-checking habit. Every time content you want to share makes you feel rage, laughter, ridicule, or even a heartwarming buzz, spend 30 seconds fact-checking. It will do you well.[2]

As emotional content online spreads, it creates spaces where misinformation will be shared and then shared again. Let's think back to what we know of the information landscape: It's controlled by algorithms and companies that want to make money. Is it any surprise, then, that the content that spreads the fastest is the content that's the most emotional? Emotional content and clickbait headlines capture our attention, and we respond. It keeps us on the page and seeing more ads. It allows misinformation to spread because it keeps people's emotions at the forefront of their response.

Common advice in many areas of our lives involves this pause. How many times are we told to write the email when we're upset but then wait to send it? Or to take a day before talking with someone to avoid saying something we regret? This is common advice we hear over and over and reminds us that responding out of emotion is often not good for our relationships. But somehow, in the emotional content of our online, social media spaces, it seems easy to forget. We leave comments that include language we wouldn't say to someone's face, or we share a news story out of emotion, because it matches our viewpoints, without verifying whether it's accurate. We can stay anonymous, or at the very least at a distance, posting on pages where no one actually knows us. This allows some people to post unkind things they wouldn't say in person.

Please know I don't advocate that you ignore your emotions or stuff them away or pretend they don't exist. As someone who has chosen to engage in professional therapy in my life, I've learned that hiding and ignoring emotions are just as unhealthy and unhelpful as overreacting. Instead, I advocate that we take the advice of therapists and counselors and pause, notice, and name our emotions. This gives us the space to decide how we want to respond. This gives us space to do some fact-checking without responding from a purely emotional place.

Admittedly, this can be hard to do. As human beings, some of us respond quickly and don't always take stock of our emotions. Others of us freeze when emotions are high and literally can't respond. Some of us choose to retreat. There's something to be said about our fight, flight, freeze responses in highly emotional situations. They can prevent us from accessing other parts of our brain, but they're normal human responses. If we're honest, we may respond in these ways when we read the news or scroll through social media. To help with all these reactions, here's an activity you can do to help you check your emotions:

First, when scrolling through social media or the news, notice your internal state and stop when you feel a strong emotion. Name the reaction you have to what you see or read. Is there a judgment or fault-finding reaction along with it? Do you think, "Those people are crazy!" or "I can't believe he said that!" or "What's wrong with them?" or "This newscaster [or news source] is terrible!" These are examples of judgments we might experience when we read or hear something that upsets us.

Next, when you notice yourself thinking those types of judgmental statements, pause and name the emotion or judgment that goes with it. If it's helpful, you can find lots of feelings charts online with a simple search. A sample feelings wheel is shown in the image on page 82. Print one off and post it somewhere you'll see it. Or keep one on your phone you can refer to regularly. As you notice your judgments and emotions, maybe you feel angry because of something happening in your city or sad about current world events. Maybe you feel happy because you see a news story about something positive happening in your community. Whatever it is, name the specific emotion you feel, even just in your mind.

Finally, reframe the events or news articles in factual language. Name the who, what, where, and when without any personal judgments. For example, "The mayor gave a speech yesterday about rent control." Or, "Yesterday it snowed six inches." Notice the focus on things that can be described absolutely, as opposed to the judgment or emotion you attached to the event. Remove any opinions you notice in the story or inferences; focus solely on facts. This factual language will also help remove yourself from the emotional response, giving you some time to decide how or whether to react.

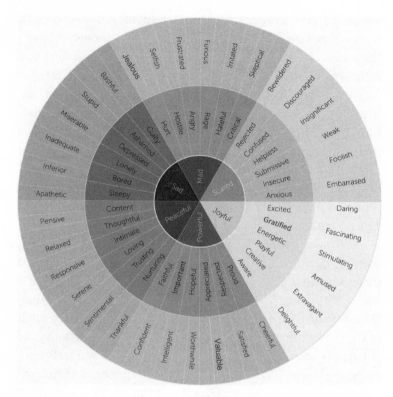

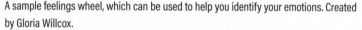

A sample feelings wheel, which can be used to help you identify your emotions. Created by Gloria Willcox.

I learned this activity in a type of therapy called dialectical behavioral therapy (DBT). The therapist had us walk through a similar activity, and I found it so helpful I've since shared it with others. These steps are adapted from skills learned in DBT called "check the facts" and "nonjudgmental mindfulness." Checking your emotions doesn't have to be a long, drawn out, emotional activity. It can be as simple as acknowledging and naming what you feel as you engage with your online spaces and reframing what you see.

And by naming your emotions and removing your own personal judgment, you'll create some separation from your immediate reaction, allowing you to calm down. This space and separation give you time to then decide how you want to respond. We can't move forward unless we acknowledge where we are and where we've been. Again, this isn't to say you won't have emotions or even that you need to change them. But by giving yourself space to notice them and reframe an event, you'll allow yourself to take a step back. To calm your body and your emotions. How many of us could benefit from pausing before reacting and responding too quickly? As someone who generally reacts quickly, I know I could use some pauses in my life to slow down.

This is counterintuitive, I know. Thinking back to what we learned about the information landscape, we know that generally these platforms aren't designed for that level of slowing down or thoughtful engagement. They thrive on reactivity. But if Christians want to be different, this is one way we can act differently in our online spaces—slowing down and bringing intentionality to our reactions. We can choose to engage in real dialogue, which requires a certain level of vulnerability that isn't necessarily supported in these online platforms. And we'll address this more later when we talk about loving our neighbors—we can choose to engage with people in person, bypassing the online spaces altogether.

A study released in 2021 by researchers in the United Kingdom showed that people who exhibit high emotional intelligence were more likely to be able to identify false information on Facebook.[3] Although this was a small study, it has something important to show us about how the practice of checking our emotions can help us in this work of being wise online in how and what we consume. Checking in with our emotions, noticing our own emotional state regularly, and being able to name our emotions are all signs of emotional intelligence. If we can continue to practice emotional intelligence, it just might help us as we move into trying to recognize false information. If we can practice being whole human beings—paying attention to our spiritual, rational, *and* emotional states of being—we may just have more of a shot at addressing all the misinformation we see in this complex information age.

REFLECTION QUESTIONS

- When scrolling through social media, what emotions do you notice inside yourself?
- Keep a list of emotions you feel over the course of a day or two when you're online—what patterns do you notice? (See exercise 4 below.)
- What might it look like to take a break from social media, at least for a time? Maybe delete some apps from your phone for a month? Author Cal Newport calls this a digital detox. Notice your emotions without the technology, and notice your emotions when you come back to it.
- Consider doing a breathing exercise when you feel your emotions getting elevated from online content. Even just three to five deep breaths can help calm your emotions. You can even find examples on YouTube to guide you through a breathing exercise.
- Thinking back to the study that showed anger is the emotion that spreads fastest online, what's the implication for Christians? Note: There's space for righteous anger when we see injustice in our world online. There are things in our world that should make us angry, but what does it look like to contribute (or not) to a general rhetoric of anger in online spaces?
- If being more emotionally intelligent could help you be wise in your online spaces and potentially help you identify misinformation, how can you grow in emotional intelligence?

EXERCISE 4: CHECKING YOUR EMOTIONS

In this chapter, we talked about checking our emotions as we engage with information online. In an environment that thrives on emotional content, the practice of checking our emotions can help slow us down and allow us to engage more wisely with online content. Try this exercise to help you notice your emotions as you spend time online. Remember that we don't need to change our emotions but simply check in and notice them.

STEP 1. Look up a feelings chart or wheel online. This can be as simple as doing a Google search for "feelings chart." Or use the one earlier in this chapter.

STEP 2. Print it out, bookmark it, or take a screenshot with your phone.

STEP 3. For several days, keep a running list of the emotions you notice when you're online (using Google, reading news, scrolling Facebook, watching videos, etc.). You can keep a list on your phone or a piece of paper. Refer to the feelings chart to name the emotions if you have trouble pinpointing the exact emotion. If you have time, also note what you were looking at when you felt the emotion.

STEP 4. At the end of the time, reflect on the emotions you listed. What patterns do you see? Are there specific apps that spark specific emotions? Or specific topics? Journal or pray over these reflections. What might God be asking you to do next? What can you learn from the emotions you noticed?

STEP 5. Get a bit more curious about those emotional reactions, and dig a bit deeper. What information can you learn from your emotions about how you engage online?

ADDITIONAL RESOURCES

Anderson, Tony, and David James Robertson. "Fake News: People with Greater Emotional Intelligence Are Better at Spotting Misinformation." The Conversation. March 22, 2021. https://thecon

versation.com/fake-news-people-with-greater-emotional-intel
ligence-are-better-at-spotting-misinformation-157265. This online article is a summary of the research study, mentioned in
this chapter, that shows people with emotional intelligence were
better able to recognize misinformation. There are some helpful
things to think about here as we reflect on what it means to check
our emotions and be more emotionally intelligent in order to slow
the spread of misinformation. This study shows that sometimes
using logic isn't enough to stop misinformation. We need to address this more holistically.

Caulfield, Mike. "Building a Fact-Checking Habit by Checking
Your Emotions." In *Web Literacy for Student Fact-Checkers*. Self-
published, 2017. https://webliteracy.pressbooks.com/chapter
/building-a-habit-by-checking-your-emotions/. Part of a longer
ebook that outlines a number of fact-checking skills, this chapter
in particular outlines the important habit of checking our emotions as part of our fact-checking toolset.

Newport, Cal. *Digital Minimalism: Choosing a Focused Life in a Noisy
World*. New York: Portfolio/Penguin, 2019. While not entirely
about checking our emotions or about fact-checking, in this
book, Newport lays out steps that help us reframe our relationship with technology and, in particular, social media, which may
in turn help our emotional state.

CHAPTER 5

Learning to Evaluate

Now comes another very practical part of this book: a number of specific fact-checking tools and techniques. I assume you read this book because your faith is important to you and is what drives you to want to be wise in online spaces. Remembering your reasons why will make you more likely to want to try some of these things. Why do you want to learn these tools? Which of those reasons are also about your faith? Naming specific reasons will help you stick with some of these practices and tools when you're online.

Additionally, I suspect that you want to have tools to help you discern what's true about all kinds of situations and issues. A lot of people of faith are drawn to these tools and the idea of addressing misinformation because they want to be truth-tellers and follow in Jesus's example of loving others well. Sharing misinformation or false information isn't loving or taking care of our neighbor or helping further the kingdom of God. These tools can help us explore the information we find online and decide what's true and what might be more questionable.

In this chapter, we'll talk about a number of different skills and tools you can use to help you be wise in online spaces, but if you don't connect them to a personal, deeper, and faith-filled purpose, when it gets hard, you might choose to skip using them. I get it. We aren't necessarily wired to stick with hard things or want to keep digging into issues that are complex. But again, now is a good time to pause and think about why you care, why you want to dig deeper on current issues, and even why you felt compelled to read this book.

I cover a number of specific tools and practices in this chapter. I'd encourage you to pick one at a time to practice. An easy way to get overwhelmed—and stop using the tools—is to try too many at once. Maybe set a goal to try one a day. Or maybe pick one and use it for a week on multiple things you see online. Regardless, I always recommend not doing too much at once. It's likely to put you into an unsustainable place where it's too hard to fact-check and tempting to stop trying. If you're tempted to feel overwhelmed by these tools, share them with a trusted friend or family member. Try them together. See what you each find. Discuss how using them changes your perspectives.

As a reminder, these tools are the middle part of the framework for consuming information wisely, which I introduced at the be-ginning of the book. Once we understand the information land-scape and the big picture, we can learn some specific tools to help us evaluate what we see, hear, and read. After we evaluate, we can decide how we want to respond, which we'll discuss in section 3.

The tools mentioned in this chapter are simply that—tools you can add to your own fact-checking tool belt. They can be used singularly or together to help you determine whether the infor-mation you find is relevant and credible. To be clear, you don't need to use every tool, every time you're online. Some will be more helpful in specific situations than others. Some will need to be used multiple times to understand a current event or issue. Other times you'll need only one. But together, these tools will give you some additional critical thinking skills as you move through your online spaces.

And as a caution, in the nature of loving our neighbors, I don't advocate using these tools in an "I told you so" way with our friends and family to try to prove a point. In my classes, I've seen people also prickle at the idea of fact-checking because someone else in their lives used it as a weapon. Someone told them, "Hey, I fact-checked this, and here's how you're wrong." As Christians, we want to practice humility and kindness when speaking truth to others, while avoiding attacking people to tell them they're wrong. Generally, people don't respond well to being told they're wrong. I encourage you to start by using these tools to help yourself understand a situation. We'll talk more about how to approach someone who believes misinformation or disinformation in a later chapter, because, yes, there are times we need to speak up with the truth of a situation.

Here are some examples of scenarios where you might want to use these tools:

- when you want to determine whether something is true or determine that it's *not* misinformation
- when you want to learn about a different perspective, that is, when you want to intentionally get out of your filter bubble to understand someone else's point of view, experiences, or values
- when you see or hear something that seems outrageous and you notice your emotions are heightened.

Can you think of other scenarios where you tried to determine whether something is true? Or times that you wish you knew how to verify something you saw or read?

It's also worth noting that there are many frameworks for fact-checking online, and you can find many videos and articles telling you how to fact-check images, news stories, and more. I'll list some of them in the resources section at the end of the chapter, but the ones we discuss in this chapter will get you started. If you find other techniques, use them! This isn't meant to be a comprehensive list of tools but rather the top few to get you started. And please know you don't need to use all these tools all the time. The more you practice them, the more you'll learn when to use which ones. Try different combinations of tools in different scenarios to see which work best. With practice, you'll find certain combinations and tools work better for certain types of scenarios.

As always, go back to noticing your emotions if you're not sure whether to dig deeper on an issue. Often the information that causes us to feel the strongest emotions (excitement, anger, outrage, etc.) are the exact things we should pay attention to and fact-check. If something seems too good to be true, it probably is and would likely be worth digging into a bit deeper. If something seems so outrageous and makes you very angry, there's a chance it's clickbait and worth considering more critically. Use your emotional reaction as a tool to help you decide when to dig deeper.

That's not to say you should fact-check only things that cause you to have an emotional reaction. Your emotions shouldn't be the only tool you use to decide when to do some fact-checking, but they can be a helpful barometer. It's a good practice to at least regularly check some of the things you engage with. This helps us get outside our filter bubblers (those bubbles again!) and echo chambers in order to learn new things. Using fact-checking tools regularly will help you be more well rounded in your understanding of the world. And as you better understand the world, you'll be more equipped to be peacemakers in our world.

You can also consider asking the Holy Spirit to help you discern what to fact-check. Consider asking the Spirit to help you pay attention to your emotions and to the events and issues that cause you to either always agree or disagree with what you find online. You might notice some trends in the promptings.

Before we go through some specific tools, it's also worth defining what I mean by "fact-checking." I tend to use this term fairly broadly to mean looking into something a bit deeper and finding the nuance of a situation. Some people will use the term to specifically mean checking the facts of a specific situation and to possibly imply that there's a right and wrong to every scenario. However, sometimes—many times—there isn't only one way to look at a situation, and fact-checking a current issue or claim may lead you to a more nuanced conclusion about an event or issue. I use the term "fact-checking" because it's easy for people to understand, but it's always worth a reminder that fact-checking doesn't always mean you'll find a black-and-white answer. Digging deeper on many topics often leads us into gray spaces, where we look at different sides of an issue to make our conclusion.

I mentioned some specific scenarios that you might want to use these tools in, but here are some specific types of content where fact-checking may also be helpful. Remember online spaces aren't a monolith—a space filled with one kind of information. There's a huge variety of the types of information you interact with, and it can be helpful to think about specific types of resources and content you might find online and on social media. Note that this is just a sampling of options. Obviously use these tools on other content as well!

Some specific types of content you might want to fact-check:

- Memes: These are images that are often shared on social media with some sort of text added across or next to them. They're often used to convey a message by combining the image with text. Some are funny and benign, but others are a commentary on current political issues and events and may need to be fact-checked.
- Quotations from leaders with no context, or sound bites on the radio: These quotations are often missing key context, and fact-checking can help you get a more nuanced understanding of the situation.
- Emotional-sounding headlines: We see these types of news headlines all the time on social media. Remember headlines of news articles are meant to catch your attention.

- Hot-button social issues in the news: Our world is full of controversial issues, and when an event happens related to one of those issues, it's worth digging a bit deeper.
- Images: Our online spaces are filled with images that have been manipulated, taken out of context, reapplied to new situations, and more. We can dig deeper to see whether the images are accurate.

What other types of content can you think of that you've fact-checked or wished you had the skills to fact-check?

Finally, as we walk through different ways to fact-check and evaluate what you find, I've chosen a number of different examples so you can see the skill in practice. Remember these are just examples and not meant to convey a specific political or social view. These are things I've seen online over the last couple of years and have found them helpful to illustrate the different skills.

As we walk through these different ways to fact-check and evaluate the things you find online, it's worth reminding us all again that this is kingdom work. Being willing to check something before sharing it is part of what God has for us—that we'd be part of finding and telling the truth, not spreading false information. I often refer to this work as discipleship work. If discipleship is about becoming more like Jesus, then seeking truth is part of that too. Like in other areas of discipleship, we can listen for the still voice of God as we do this fact-checking work. That's not to say that we should replace our truth-seeking only with the voice of the Spirit but that when we combine our willingness to seek truth through fact-checking with our ability to listen to the Spirit, we're much more holistic in how we pay attention to the world around us.

And as with all discipleship work, we need to be familiar with the Spirit's voice. In all the areas we try to be more like Jesus—growing in the fruit of the Spirit in all areas of our lives—we need to practice listening to his voice. If we don't recognize it, we may miss his promptings. As we learn to listen, his voice will also help us as we engage with fact-checking. In the past, I've heard the ministry leaders say, "As you listen to someone, listen to their words with one ear and to the Spirit with the other" as a way to not speak into someone's life without thinking. We can adopt a similar posture in our online spaces: listening to the Holy Spirit but also paying attention to our fact-checking skills. We'll be able to combine his promptings with what we find and learn, allowing us to see both the spiritual and physical parts of our world.

USE FACT-CHECKING WEBSITES

One of the easiest and first things you can do to check something is to use fact-checking websites. There are a number of organizations online that are already doing fact-checking work, and we can take advantage of them. Websites like Snopes, Politifact, and FactCheck.org regularly check claims, images, rumors, quotations, and other current events. They can often be a great first stop on your fact-checking journey when you hear something that sounds unusual or questionable. They're especially helpful for sound-bite types of information we catch in a headline or on the radio.

Usually when I bring up these sites in a faith and fake news class, someone almost immediately asks, "But aren't these sites biased?" or says, "I heard that Snopes [or whatever site] has a liberal [or conservative] bias." We'll talk more about bias later in this chapter, but it's worth mentioning now that everything has bias. People have bias and people create these sites (along with most everything else online). Yes, you may find some bias in these sites, but the type of bias tends to be less about one specific fact-check being biased and more about the overall volume of fact-checks being about a specific political party or issue.

That being said, these websites are incredibly helpful. The good fact-checking websites will cite the sources they used so you know why they came to the conclusion they did, rating something true or false. They'll likely also provide you with additional context about the rumor, quote, and so on. Most of these websites hire journalists or other professional fact-checkers who have skills specifically in verifying and finding truth, and while, yes, you may notice some bias, you can generally trust that you'll at least get more information than you had before. You can use their list of sources to continue looking at the issue if you want.

For example, Politifact (www.politifact.com), which is owned by the Poynter Institute, a nonprofit school of journalism, will give each fact-check a rating on a truth-o-meter indicating where the claim falls on a spectrum from "pants on fire" to "half true" to "mostly true" to "true." (Hint: many fact-checks on this website fall in the middle somewhere.) In addition to a quick snapshot on the truth-o-meter, Politifact will publish a short explanation of why they gave the rating. But the most important part of any good fact-check like this is a list of sources to back up their conclusion. They list the tweets, news stories, and other sites that were used in the fact-check. You can also see who wrote the fact-check and their credentials, whether they've worked in journalism or somewhere else, and how long they've worked for Politifact. All these things give you a lot more information about the initial claim and how it's been researched.

I point all these things out because of the pushback I've gotten about websites like these and because it's important to look past any initial reaction we have to these kinds of websites. Remember those emotions? I've talked to folks who have tried to use fact-checking websites in the past but either saw facts they didn't like or were told that the sites were biased, and now they don't trust the work being done.

Good fact-checking websites will often move beyond a binary of true or false when checking a claim and give you the nuance and sources that help you understand the fact-check and, more importantly, the situation of the claim or rumor. I encourage people to use these kinds of sites because we don't need to re-invent the wheel. If someone has already looked into a news source or claim, we don't necessarily need to do additional digging. We can start with what they found and go from there.

I recently used some fact-checking websites to check a claim I saw online. Someone posted on Facebook that the platform was no longer allowing people to post the Lord's Prayer. Maybe you, too, saw this. The post basically said that it was against Facebook's policies to post the Lord's Prayer. Admittedly, there was also a bit of an emotional plea along with the post asking people to keep posting the prayer. Instead of reacting to what I saw, I hopped out of Facebook and did a quick fact-check search to see whether this was true. I simply searched Google for "Facebook Lord's Prayer policies." Immediately, my top result was a fact-check website from Reuters explaining that this claim was false.[1] It included quotations from Facebook's parent company, Meta, saying that this wasn't true and their policy didn't prohibit the posting of the Lord's Prayer.

As always, I don't want to pick on the person who posted this or anyone who has believed something like this in the past. I simply want to point out how often we see this kind of claim and how easy it is to repost it without verifying it. Remember that appeal to emotions? False information often not only preys on our emotions but may also come into conflict with our values. When we have that emotional response, we can react quickly and potentially without verifying the information, which is exactly what those platforms want.

I also suspect that, depending on someone's preconceived notion about Facebook or other social media platforms, seeing a post like that simply confirms what they already believe: that the platforms are somehow censoring information or not trustworthy. Regardless, posts like these are a good reminder to do quick Google searches or check fact-checking websites before sharing. You may find yourself surprised at what you find and be able to stop misinformation from spreading.

REFLECTION QUESTIONS

- Have you tried using a fact-checking website, such as Politifact or FactCheck.org? What did you notice?
- Try going to a fact-checking website and look through some of the fact-checks. What do you notice about your emotional state?
- Content we see online is often impacted by the creator's values. When you look at a fact-checking website, can you identify the values at play in the specific fact-checks? Either by the original statement or image being fact-checked or by the language used in the fact-check itself?

EXERCISE 5.1: FACT-CHECKING WEBSITES

In order to try using this skill, start by simply using fact-checking websites. This exercise will help you practice using these sites and reflect on what you find. Sometimes looking at these websites can cause people to have strong emotional reactions based on whether they agree or disagree with what they find. Consider asking the Holy Spirit for an open mind before you start this exercise, keeping your mind open to what you read even if it surprises you.

STEP 1. Go to a fact-checking website: Politifact, Snopes, or Fact Check.org.

STEP 2. Scroll through the types of claims they fact-check. Do they just fact-check claims made in the news? Do they look at images? What can you tell about the information they verify?

STEP 3. Click on a fact-check that looks interesting to you or surprises you. Read through how they came to their conclusion.

STEP 4. Reflect on what you see on the website. What surprises you? What upsets you? Be curious about your own reactions. Why might you be responding that way?

STEP 5. Reflect on how you can use these websites the next time you come across something to fact-check. Consider bookmarking the site so it's easier to get back to.

LATERAL READING

Another step you can take to dig deeper on a current issue is something called "lateral reading." Yes, this phrase is jargony, but stay with me. Lateral reading is a technique used by professional fact-checkers and involves a bit of patience and digging. This technique is helpful when you come across information published by an organization or author you're unfamiliar with. It can also be helpful to learn more about organizations or people you've heard of but haven't taken the time to get the full context.

Think about a time you saw someone post something online but you didn't recognize the organization that was hosting the information. Maybe you saw something about coronavirus research but didn't recognize the medical organization that posted the information. Or maybe your friend shared an article from a doctor you've never heard of. Or possibly there was commentary on social media about a current event, but you didn't recognize the news organization posting it.

Instead of taking that information at face value and reading it or watching it immediately, you can use this tool of lateral reading. Before reading or watching the content, open a new tab in your browser (on your phone or computer) and search for the organization or author. If they're an individual, you may find their social media page or LinkedIn profile. High-profile individuals may even have a Wikipedia page about them. If it's an organization, there may also be a Wikipedia page about them or other sites that share more information. Sometimes the person or organization has been in the news, and you can see more information from the newspaper or news site. What do these other, secondary sources tell you about the creator(s) or sponsor of the information? Are they trustworthy? If you find the author's LinkedIn page and there's nothing about their credentials, that may be a red flag. A Wikipedia page may tell you whether the organization or author has any controversies surrounding them.

Lateral reading is basically taking the time to explore what you can about the creator and their credentials before you take what they say at face value. It can provide you with context that informs whether you want to read or watch the original content or move on past. It can also give you context as you engage with the original content.

Let's look at a couple of examples in the wild.

Soon after the COVID-19 pandemic was declared in 2020 and many states and cities within the United States went into lockdown as a way to flatten the curve, it wasn't uncommon to find YouTube videos of various health-care professionals making statements about the pandemic, lockdowns, and so on. Some of these professionals agreed with the messaging that was put out by the Centers for Disease Control and Prevention, the World Health Organization, and other public health organizations. But some health-care professionals disagreed, and it also wasn't uncommon to find their videos, blogs, and articles circulating on social media.

In April 2020, someone in one of my circles posted a video on social media of Drs. Dan Erickson and Artin Massihi claiming that the shelter-in-place orders were unnecessary and that infection rates weren't as high as predicted. This was counter to some of the news I had read, so I was curious. But instead of diving in and watching their video, I looked up the doctors first. I wondered, who are they? Where did they get their degrees? What kind of medicine do they practice? In this case, I discovered they were emergency medicine specialists and co-owned Accelerated Urgent Care in Bakersfield, California. They aren't infectious disease doctors or epidemiologists. Once I learned more about their background, I had a few options: Should I watch the video, knowing that these weren't doctors who specialize in infectious diseases? Could they still have valuable information on the pandemic? Or should I move on and focus on health-care professionals who specialize in fields relevant to the pandemic, such as epidemiology?

That's the point of lateral reading—to give you the context of the information and decide how you want to move forward. As we discussed earlier, it's incredibly easy for people to put information online. But sometimes it's up to us to explore their backgrounds a bit more before diving into the information. This doesn't mean you can't or shouldn't engage with the material, but sometimes giving yourself some context will help you decide how to move forward or whether you want to.

Here's another example. Someone I know posted an article from a website called LifeSite News, which I had never heard of. Before reading the article posted I did two things: (1) I found the website's "About" page to see what information they said about themselves; and (2) I googled "lifesite news." The "About" page told me that the site is a nonprofit and was originally started by Campaign Life Coalition, which is a Canadian national, pro-life organization. My Google search led me to the Wikipedia page about the site, which told me that it's been flagged multiple times for spreading misinformation.

With this additional information about the website that hosts the article that was posted, I can then decide how to move forward. This is all helpful context to understand the information on the site and the perspective they might bring to the news article I saw posted. Is this information I want to engage with? Will it help me understand a different perspective? Knowing that the content has been flagged in the past for being untrue, how can I fact-check any specific claims I read for accuracy?

Again, just because you find out more context on a given source doesn't mean you have to immediately throw it out or immediately read it. Instead, ask yourself, "How does this additional context help me move forward in my understanding of the original source, article, video, and so on?" Sometimes you may decide to skip the content altogether. Other times you may decide to read or watch anyway, with the purpose of thinking about a different perspective. This is another area we can invite the Holy Spirit into our online habits. How do you feel prompted to move forward?

Some of you do this all the time already. What I find so helpful about this tool is that it allows us to understand a bigger picture of where information comes from. It can also help us manage our emotions. For example, if you see an article that makes you angry, but instead of responding immediately you do some lateral reading and find out that the creator is widely reported to be sharing false information, it may help you manage your anger, realizing that the creator isn't credible.

REFLECTION QUESTIONS

- Have you ever completely paused your browsing online or on social media to stop and research a writer or organization? What did you find?
- How does the skill of laterally reading the news and getting more context compare to the ways you read and interpret the Bible? Do you also seek out the broader context of the Bible passages you read?
- How might applying a broader context to information (learning more about the creator or hosting organization) inform your understanding of the information? How might it result in a different emotion and reaction?

EXERCISE 5.2: LATERAL READING

Like all of the tools in this chapter, the more you practice, the easier they get. Use this exercise to practice looking at the context of a source and lateral reading.

STEP 1. Go to your social media site of choice: Twitter, Instagram, Facebook, and so on. If you don't use any social media platforms, do a Google search for a topic or issue you're interested in.

STEP 2. Scroll through your social media feed or search and look for an unfamiliar name or organization that has posted information.

STEP 3. Perform a Google search for that person or organization. Look for a LinkedIn page or Wikipedia page. You may even find some news articles talking about the person or organization.

STEP 4. Look at a couple different sites, and compare what you find. You might even look at their own "About" pages to see what they say about themselves. Do they list their purpose or how they're funded?

STEP 5. What did you learn about the context of the creator, author, or organization? What surprises you? How does learning more about the person or organization help you understand the bigger context of the information? Would you continue looking at their content or stop? Why?

STEP 6. Reflect on how this exercise changes your perspective on a particular piece of news or content creator. Also, reflect on what you might do differently the next time you try lateral reading.

LEARNING FROM EXPERTS

Related to lateral reading is the ability to recognize who are experts on particular topics. I hear skepticism about this all the time when talking with churches and congregations. Questions like "How do I know whether someone is an expert?" or "Why does it seem like everyone is an expert?" or "Why do I think so-and-so is an expert on a topic but my friend thinks someone else is the expert?" There is so much confusion about finding and listening to experts.

I talked about this briefly in chapter 2, but it's worth looking at a few specific examples as we talk about specifically fact-checking sources. With the proliferation of online information, it's easy for anyone to post and share about (almost) any topic. They can create websites that make them look like experts. Additionally, with the ease in which people create information, it can feel like somehow everyone is an expert.

Let's go back to the video example described in the lateral reading section. Drs. Erickson and Massihi are medical professionals. I can look them up online with lateral reading and with some digging find out more about where they went to medical school and their medical credentials. I can find out that they practice at an organization called Accelerated Urgent Care.

But here's where things get tricky and possibly confusing. They're known for their video at the beginning of the pandemic about the rate of disease and whether lockdowns were worth it. Yet they don't have any credentials relating to infectious disease. Are they medical experts? Yes, at least from what I can tell online. Are they experts in pandemic-level spread of disease? No, not from what I can tell online. Specifically with regard to health information, we need to be careful to not equate medical degree with expert on X, Y, or Z medical topic. When we have heart disease, we see a cardiologist, not a foot doctor. Medical providers specialize for a reason, and we can use their expertise to help us address our health concerns. But we want to make sure they're experts in what we need them to be experts in.

I can't help but wonder whether that's part of why the COVID-19 pandemic has created so much division in our culture and, if we're honest, division with our families and relationships. People look to different experts on the topic, and we end up with a lot of different opinions about what to do within our own communities. I also wonder whether we all lay our own values on top of the information we see from different experts, adding to the confusion.

Personally, I've found it helpful to follow epidemiologists and infectious disease doctors with regard to the pandemic, not politicians or even the news sometimes. I go straight to the websites of scientists who are experts on pandemics and epidemiology (after lateral reading about them!). Some have specifically set up social media accounts or created podcasts in order to help people understand the disease more thoroughly on platforms that are more accessible than a scholarly research journal. Eventually this current pandemic will pass (we hope!), and there will be another current event in which we'll need to evaluate whether someone is an expert. I'd encourage you, whenever possible, to go straight to the source. But also think very carefully about what makes someone an expert in their field.

So, what are some things that make someone an expert? Here are some questions I teach my college students to ask about the experts they see talking about current events and issues:

- Does the person have a degree or certification in what they talk about? Can you tell where from?
- Do they have work experience in what they talk about?
- What else have they written on the topic? Remember when it comes to medical information, writing about medicine in general isn't the same as writing about a specific type of medicine.
- Do they seem to cite their sources from other scholars and experts?

- If you google their name, what else can you find out about them? (Not just from their own website!) Have they been part of anything controversial? Use that lateral reading skill to learn more about them!
- If they're associated with a current event or situation, how close are they to the event? Were they there as an eyewitness?

Likely you use similar questions every day to evaluate whether someone is expert enough for a service you use or other types of things you seek out. For example, we might seek out a general handyman to do small jobs around our house, but if we want to remodel our bathroom, we might try to find a contractor or plumber who specializes in home bathrooms. You likely have a series of questions you ask these people to determine whether they're experts in what you're looking for. Similarly, we need to ask questions of the people providing us with information to determine whether their expertise matches our information needs.

Finally, one last reminder to notice your emotions as you research whether someone is an expert. Be honest with yourself about whether they're an expert. I've seen people agree so strongly with an expert's opinion, because it either matches their values or confirms their opinion, that they ignore any warning signs that the expert might not really be an expert.

REFLECTION QUESTIONS

- Think over the past two weeks. Did you read any content where the source inferred a person was an expert in a specific field because they had a certain type of credential, such as a PhD or MD? Was the credential specific to the topic being discussed?
- In the past, how have you determined whether someone was an expert on their topic? Think about both the social issues you've researched (e.g., homelessness) and the everyday things (e.g., finding a repairperson).

- Can you think of times you assumed someone was an expert just because their conclusion matched your own opinion or values?

EXERCISE 5.3: FINDING EXPERTS

In the last few years, we've seen a lot of confusion about who the experts are on a lot of different current events and social issues. It can often feel like everyone is following their own set of experts that match their opinions. Use this exercise to practice looking at someone's credentials and reflect honestly on whether they're an expert on their topic.

STEP 1. Look at a news article from the last day or two, from any news source.

STEP 2. Look for the people related to the article. This could be the author or anyone quoted or mentioned in the article.

STEP 3. If there are people mentioned in the article or quoted, what kind of experts do they claim to be?

STEP 4. See what you can find out about at least one of the people related to the article. Use the questions listed in this section to help you.

STEP 5. Reflect honestly on what you find. Is the person actually an expert? Why or why not? How does that change your view of what you read?

FIND THE ORIGINAL SOURCE

Another fact-checking tool involves a bit of digging, too, but in a slightly different way. It involves finding an original source or going upstream. There are a number of times this can be a help-ful skill to practice, and we'll talk about a few of them. But before we do that, spend a minute or two reflecting on times you've reacted to a news source or other piece of information simply from the headline. If you're like me, you've read the headlines of articles and assumed you knew what was going on from that headline, without actually reading the entire article. This is a perfect example of not going to the original source and instead relying on a very short summary of an event.

One time this might be helpful is when you see articles that say something along the lines of "In a recent study . . ." followed by a summary of that study. Or "so-and-so organization just re-leased a study. . . ." This has been especially common during the coronavirus pandemic but was common prior to that as well. As researchers, scientists, social scientists, and others conduct studies on everything from viruses to human behavior to child development, it's not uncommon to see the results of these stud-ies listed in the news or other online platforms.

On the one hand, it can be helpful to read the summary of the article from whatever news source you look at. Likely the news source is at a level that's understandable to you, whereas the original study is often in a scholarly or peer-reviewed jour-nal, written for other experts in the field. The original studies are often written in high-level jargon that can be hard for some of us to follow. And at the same time, sometimes it can be more helpful to go back to the original source instead of relying on rereporting. (But also remember in chapter 2 when we talked about knowing our own limitations. Just because we find a scholarly article as the original source doesn't mean we can in-terpret it appropriately.)

This also happens with events reported in the news. One news outlet runs the original story, and then other outlets rereport it. This can result in a massive game of telephone. Remember the game you might have played as a child, where you whisper something in one kid's ear who then whispers it into another kid's ear? Eventually the original message is so mangled it no longer resembles the original.

The same thing happens with information. The more times something is rereported or repeated, the more likely that the original context and message will be mangled. Think about how this even plays out in our conversations. Someone at work says, "I was reading an article about . . . that said. . . ." Or at a family dinner someone mentions the news article they saw recently and tries to summarize it. These are all normal points of conversation and not things we generally fact-check. We don't need to find the original source or article of everything people mention, but it can be helpful when (again) our emotions are triggered. If someone says, "Can you believe this article I read!" and we feel outraged with them, it might be worth tracking down the article they're talking about to make sure it says what they or we think.

This can also happen with quotations from world leaders or others in the news. We hear sound bites on the radio or read a two-sentence quotation from an interview. It might be helpful to find the transcript of the entire interview before jumping to conclusions or find an unedited video of the whole conversation. The media makes it easy to pull quotations out of context and make it look like someone said something they didn't. Tracking down the original quotation or source is a valuable skill that takes practice and isn't one many people engage in.

But what does this look like in real life? How can we practice finding the original source out in the wild of social media?

In my personal life, I came across an example in 2020. Someone posted a link to a news article with the headline "Antifa Rioters Deface World War II and Lincoln Memorials on National Mall." Accompanying the headline was a picture of a small, beige building absolutely covered in graffiti and swear words.

This was right after the murder of George Floyd in Minneapolis, when unrest took over many major cities in the United

States. I was struck by this image because of how it was paired with a headline about the memorials, and yet the picture itself wasn't of the Lincoln or World War II memorials. In fact, having visited those memorials in Washington, DC, in the past, I didn't remember seeing a building like this at all. When I saw this image, I also thought, "If this happened, why am I not hearing about it more widely on the news? Is it just the news sources I'm reading? Am I not engaging with news sources that would report this? Or is there something else going on that I've missed?"

So out of curiosity I clicked on the headline. It took me to a website I didn't normally follow: American Greatness. The header on the news story was the same image I had seen on social media, but as I scanned the page, this sentence jumped out at me: "Multiple historic landmarks in Washington D.C. were vandalized by far-left domestic terrorists on Sunday night, as reported by CNN."[2] CNN was hyperlinked. To be honest, I didn't even read the rest of the story on American Greatness because I wanted to get to the original source—the root of the story. So I clicked on the link for CNN.

That took me to another news story on CNN's website with a very different image and headline. On CNN, the headline was "Famed Monuments Defaced after Night of Unrest," and as I scrolled through, I found a picture of the Lincoln Memorial in the background with a smaller structure in the forefront of the picture that had graffiti that said, "YALL NOT TIRED YET?"

Yes, there was graffiti, but it looked nothing like the image I had originally seen on social media. One structure and only one sentence. It also included a shot of the Lincoln Memorial, so I was more convinced that this was the original image of the graffiti at the monuments. And I noticed in the story a link to a tweet by the National Park Service for the National Mall. I realized that tweet was likely part of the original source, reported by CNN. So I went to their tweet and found a few images of the monuments with some graffiti. The graffiti included a few sentences but, again, nothing like the image originally posted on social media. The tweet accompanying the photos said, "In the wake of last night's demonstrations, there are numerous instances of vandalism to sites around the National Mall. For generations the Mall has been our nation's premier civic gathering space for non-violent demonstrations, and we ask individuals to carry on that tradition" (@NationalMallNPS, May 31, 2020).

Finally, I had found the original source of the graffiti left on the memorials in the National Mall. A few things stood out to me in this original tweet image:

- The text of the original tweet didn't mention Antifa (which was the leading part of the headline by American Greatness).
- The images were actually of the memorials and included a lot less graffiti than the image I saw originally.

Now, I'm not saying graffiti or vandalism is okay. But what I found so interesting about this scenario was that the original images were so different from what was being passed around social media. And the headlines and images on social media were much more emotional than this original tweet and included a lot of triggering language and swear words. The images weren't of the actual event. These are the exact kinds of scenarios that are worth a bit more investigation before reacting. When I saw this story posted, I couldn't help but wonder whether someone posted it to social media out of emotion before pausing to do any fact-checking. I was also reminded of the emotional nature of many online sources and how many platforms purposely create misleading headlines or post emotional images in order to get our attention and our clicks.

Finding the original source of a news story or current event helps us react to what actually happens, not how it's rereported or how a media platform wants us to see it. We have a choice to intentionally dig deeper. Yes, it takes time. But it ensures we react to an actual event, not a mere interpretation of it. There are times when reading analysis of events is helpful and finding trusted voices on current issues is incredibly important. For example, it's okay to rely on expert analysis on complex topics. But it's also important to notice whether the posts on social media just create an emotional response that might lead to the spread of misinformation.

My example of finding the original source is mostly tracing a line of images, but you can do this with news stories as well. As I mentioned at the beginning of this section, you might also notice this in news stories where they refer to other studies or even other news stories. If you look online, many times these will be linked. Use those links to your advantage to see how far back you can go to the original information.

As we wrap up this section on finding the original source, it's worth mentioning that this is similar to what many biblical scholars and pastors do as they look at specific Bible passages. They go back to the original text, analyze the Greek or Hebrew of the text, and think about the passages in light of what was originally written. They don't automatically apply a current lens to something that was written thousands of years ago, and we're often better for their scholarship. Likewise, we have the opportunity every day to look at the original event and how it was portrayed before immediately making assumptions about what it means and how we should respond.

REFLECTION QUESTIONS

- When have you tried digging deeper to an original source? How did it go? How did you know you found the original source?
- If you've found an original source for something, did it bring clarity or make it harder to understand the issue (as in the case of finding a scholarly research article on a topic)? What did you do if you didn't understand?

- About what topics might you be less likely to try to find the original source? Why? What might it look like to try anyway?

EXERCISE 5.4: FINDING AN ORIGINAL SOURCE

This skill is often referred to as "going upstream" and is an important practice as we learn to fact-check. We want to make sure we respond to the original information as opposed to a later interpretation of it, whenever possible. Use this exercise to practice finding an original source.

For this exercise, I encourage you to do something similar as I outlined in the section. The next time you notice an article that mentions "a study" or "originally reported by . . ." try going to that study or other website. If you're online, these things will almost always be hyperlinked, making it easier to find them. If they aren't linked, try doing a Google search to find it.

After you've practiced going upstream, reflect on the following:

- How does finding the original source change my perspective on the event or issue?
- Does this change my emotional reaction?
- Was this hard to do? What might stop me from doing so again in the future?

RECOGNIZING BIAS

This could be one of the most important parts of evaluating information online and helping you distinguish truth in your online spaces. We can't talk about fact-checking and misinformation without addressing, at least in part, the role bias plays in our online spaces. Like checking our emotions, this tool is less of a step-by-step set of rules and more of a practice of paying attention to the things we find in our online spaces, including our internal state.

Sometimes people equate bias with information that they disagree with, or even information that isn't true. But finding bias in information doesn't automatically mean that information (video, article, etc.) is a lie or untrue. Bias is "an inclination of temperament or outlook," especially "a personal and sometimes unreasoned judgment" about other people—what we often call "prejudice."[3] Bias has to do with beliefs and values, not just facts. This shows up in a lot of different ways in our online spaces, but the two worth mentioning are media bias and our own personal biases.

As we talked about in chapter 1, algorithms keep us in filter bubbles and echo chambers, and these filter bubbles are created from many of our own personal browsing habits. Additionally, our personal biases inform how we see the world, especially our implicit biases—the biases we don't know we have. In the last few years, I've reflected on how these implicit biases may impact the way we search online, the people or organizations we follow on social media, the language we use to find what we look for, and more. Basically, I've explored how the ways we see the world impact our ways of engaging online and in turn continue to keep us in those filter bubbles.

Then once we layer on media bias and the ways in which organizations and others experience bias, it gets complicated. If we practice noticing and paying attention to these biases, we can practice wisdom online. We'll briefly look at both our personal, confirmation bias and media bias. Again, this is less about a specific tool that you follow step-by-step but more about noticing the world around us as well as our internal state. Remember that concept of understanding the big picture of the information landscape before we dive into specifics? This is similar.

PERSONAL BIAS AND CONFIRMATION BIAS

"Bias" is becoming a bit of a hot-button word in our news consumption, and I want to be careful in this section, as I'm not a psychologist. However, our personal biases intersect with our information consumption in a number of ways that are worth exploring as we look at fact-checking. There are a number of experts we can look to in this area to help us reflect on how our own personal biases may impact both what we see in our online spaces and how we react to it.

It's important to acknowledge that we all have biases. We're human and have our own set of life experiences, families of origin, education, and culture that contribute to how we see the world and the bias we experience. These aren't all bad but just a reality of who we are as human beings. You may have heard the terms "implicit bias" and "explicit bias." Implicit biases are the ones we aren't aware of, the ones that live in our subconscious. Explicit biases are the ones that are outwardly facing, that are expressed directly. Both types of bias show up in our lives in different ways, and both intersect with what we do in our online spaces, most notably through confirmation bias.

Confirmation bias is "the tendency to process information by looking for, or interpreting, information that is consistent with one's existing beliefs. This biased approach to decision making is largely unintentional and often results in ignoring inconsistent information."[4] This is where our biases can largely impact how we evaluate and interpret what we find online. Fact-checking is helpful, but we also have our personal biases vying for our attention and often winning out.

Eli Pariser puts it this way:

The filter bubble tends to dramatically amplify confirmation bias—in a way, it's designed to. Consuming information that conforms to our idea of the world is easy and pleasurable; consuming information that challenges us to think in new ways or question our assumptions is frustrating and difficult. This is why partisans of one political stripe tend not to consume the media of another. As a result, an information

environment built on click signals will favor content that sup-
ports our existing notions about the world over content that
challenges them.[5]

The ways in which our online platforms are constructed have the
ability to reinforce the biases we already have. We can easily seek
out information that confirms our own biases, once again missing information from other perspectives. I often encourage people in my classes to examine their own biases and reflect on how
they see the world. If we can learn to recognize our own biases
and how they might impact the way we look for information,
we'll be taking a step toward being wiser in our online spaces.

In "Moral Combat," an episode of the podcast *Hidden Brain*,
host Shankar Vedantam talks with psychologist Dr. Linda Skitka
about how our moral convictions may also impact how we take
in information about the topics we feel are morally right or
wrong. "When we are convinced something is morally correct,
it becomes difficult for us to hear views that clash with ours,
difficult to have conversations with people who disagree with
us and difficult to make compromises."[6] Dr. Skitka goes on to
explain that many issues in America that we might talk about
as political issues are often rooted within people's moral convictions on right and wrong. And when we're faced with information about the things we see as right or wrong, we'll have a
harder time listening to views different from our own.

How does this relate to fake news and (mis)information?
Knowing these things and being aware of how our brains work
is incredibly helpful in evaluating information. I suspect as
Christians we all have a number of issues we feel particularly
strongly about and likely see those issues through a moral lens.
If the research shows that we're less likely to make compromises
or listen to other perspectives on moral issues, how might that
affect the way we interact with other people? How might that
affect how we interact with information about those topics?

Think about some current social issues that you feel have a clear right or wrong to them. Maybe it's abortion or gun control or immigration. Now imagine purposely seeking out a perspective different from your own on the topic. Hard to even imagine doing so? If you find it difficult to think about pursuing those perspectives, according to Dr. Skitka, you're not alone.

Please know that I'm not saying you need to give up your moral or Christian convictions. But understanding how our biases work—how our brains work—is so helpful for us as we engage with information. We may be blind to the nuances of an issue or a current event if we only look for the right and wrong sides or focus on the side we agree with. Remember to check your emotions; they may be a good indicator of whether you're stuck in black-and-white thinking or in your own biases.

MEDIA BIAS

In addition to thinking about how our own biases impact our online spaces, the other thing I often hear people complain about is how the media is biased, and I don't disagree with them. Many media and news outlets demonstrate bias. But what I also notice is that people often mean that the media outlets or stories they disagree with are biased. Or they don't go into what they mean by biased. And as always, painting things in black-and-white terms (e.g., "this news outlet is biased!") isn't very helpful. Part of evaluating sources and information online is also recognizing the bias that might be in whatever source you listen to, watch, read, and so on.

As we talked about in the previous section, people have bias. And people write for major news and media outlets. However, it's important to note that most major news sources do have ethics codes that help them create journalism that's as unbiased as possible. For example, the *New York Times* has standards and ethics codes that guide the integrity and reporting of the newspaper. Likewise, the *Wall Street Journal* includes a section on their website about their newsroom standards and ethics. However, we'd be naive to assume that everything you read from these large reputable news sources is 100 percent bias-free.

Instead, I encourage us all to recognize and acknowledge bias in the media we consume. We'll likely never find news or online information that's 100 percent neutral. That's unlikely and unrealistic given that we as humans experience our set of biases and, as we discussed earlier, there's also bias in the algorithms that govern our online spaces. And as always, it's worth reiterating that bias in news sources also doesn't mean untrue. Sometimes when I hear people complain about how the news is biased, I wonder whether they say that because either they disagree with the content or they believe the content to be false.

However, there are a couple of tools you can use to help you recognize and determine bias in your online spaces. But before we talk about them, it's helpful to remember that these are tools, also created by humans. They're also not perfect and shouldn't be used to shame others for the sources they read or watch. They're a starting point for you to reflect on where you get your news and the bias that may be in your sources.

This first one comes from a website called AllSides. This website rates media outlets according to political bias, as seen in the image on page 117. The website also shows the same story from multiple media outlets side by side so you can see how different media report on the same event or issue.

I find a chart like this helpful in order to better balance my own news consumption. If I notice I read news from only one column, I try to balance that by picking news sources from a different column. Note that this chart specifically rates bias and not credibility. This particular tool uses an editorial board with people from across the political spectrum to rate news sources against a variety of types of bias. Because they focus on bias and not con-

This chart from AllSides is helpful for identifying media bias. AllSides Media Bias Chart™, copyright AllSides.com. Used with permission.

tent, some of the sources rated may run stories that have less credibility than others or are focused more on opinions than facts. Looking at a chart like this also runs the risk of implying that news sources down the center are the best places to get your news. Again, there's a difference between bias and accurate reporting. A news outlet can have a particular bias but still have accurate reporting of an event. We want to try to read or watch a variety of sources that are rooted in facts, not necessarily opinions.

Another media bias chart worth looking at is created by Ad Fontes Media. You can find it by searching for Ad Fontes media bias chart. It includes hundreds of news sources and charts them based on their political leaning and how reliable the reporting is. They look at whether the majority of the content includes original and fact-based reporting compared to misleading, opinion-based, or incomplete reporting. They use an in-depth methodology to rate and chart all kinds of sources from newspapers to podcasts. Like the AllSides chart, I encourage people to use this chart as a reflection tool to build nuance into their news consumption and not as black-and-white rules about what to read or watch.

Both these charts can be very useful in helping us recognize bias. When I read about some sort of current, viral event, I sometimes like to look at these charts and pick out a news source that's different from the one I was reading. I see what other sources say and notice the type of language they use to talk about the same event. AllSides.com is particularly good at showing different headlines side by side. I'd encourage you to use these charts to help you identify additional news sources to explore. Compare their headlines, compare the language used by different media outlets, and compare the ways they talk about leaders from different political parties.

Again, I don't think we should use these charts to imply that there's a black-and-white perspective on a current issue or that everything you read in the news is fact or fiction. Or even that all news sources can be squarely placed in a conservative or liberal biased side. But rather, they're really helpful for us to notice and evaluate the bias we might see in our news sources. As Christians, this can help us engage more thoroughly in the world. If we take the time to read multiple news sources, we can get a more holistic understanding of the events. And by understanding the world more holistically, we can better decide how we want to engage.

REFLECTION QUESTIONS

- When you read or watch news, can you identify any bias in the content or of the person presenting it? If not, how can you grow in this skill?
- How do you respond to information you disagree with or goes against your beliefs? Or are you willing to engage with information from sources that may have views or biases different from yours? If you do, how does that impact your understanding of other people, issues, and so on?
- Do you have personal relationships with anyone who holds different social, political, or faith views? How might talking with them inform your understanding of your own views or help shine a light on your own biases?

EXERCISE 5.5: RECOGNIZING BIAS

In this section, we talked about a couple of different places we might see bias. Being able to recognize bias can impact the way we interact with others and our online spaces. Use this exercise to reflect on bias and how it might impact the way you see the world.

STEP 1. Listen to the episode of the *Hidden Brain* podcast, "Mind Reading 2.0: The Double Standard," available online: https://hiddenbrain.org/podcast/the-double-standard/. You'll hear psychologist Emily Pronin discuss different aspects of how our brains work and how we see ourselves compared to how we see other people.

STEP 2. Reflect on what areas you might have some double standards about your own biases compared to the biases you assume others have. There are many examples given in the podcast to help you get started. Are there particular issues on which you're more likely to have these double standards?

STEP 3. Reflect on how your own biases might impact the way you search or interact with information online. Are you more inclined to read only certain types of sources? Do you find yourself agreeing with certain conclusions but not others? How might that impact what you think is true when you fact-check?

FACT AND OPINION

Finally, in this section it's worth briefly mentioning the difference between fact and opinion. Yes, I know this may feel a bit juvenile; many of us probably did fact-or-opinion exercises in elementary or middle school. But as we evaluate information, it's extremely important to be able to recognize the difference. This isn't actually a tool per se, but, like the skill of checking our emotions or recognizing bias, we need to practice the skill of knowing the difference between fact and opinion. As we've seen, so much information travels online through emotions. It's easy for this to happen if we focus on content that's opinion-based as opposed to fact-based.

This may seem obvious to you, and you may think you already know the difference. However, a survey by the Pew Research Center in 2018 showed that many adults struggle to distinguish between fact and opinion. They showed over five thousand adults ten statements, five opinions and five facts, and asked the participants to rate the statements as fact or opinion. "The main portion of the study, which measured the public's ability to distinguish between five factual statements and five opinion statements, found that a majority of Americans correctly identified at least three of the five statements in each set. But this result is only a little better than random guesses. Far fewer Americans got all five correct, and roughly a quarter got most or all wrong." Interestingly, participants were also more likely to label facts as opinions if they went against their political persuasion.[7] You can look up the statements on the Pew Research website and try for yourself. Can you tell the difference between the facts and opinions? It's also worth noting that participants struggled to tell the difference depending on how the statement lined up with their political views. Once again, our own opinions and biases can make it more difficult to evaluate information.

Remember, at the core, facts can be proved true or false. Opinions can't. I know this sounds basic, but again, with so much information available to us, it's worth pausing regularly and asking ourselves, "Is this a fact or an opinion?" Facts answer the who, what, where, when of a situation or issue. For example, if a politician gives a speech, the facts are where, when, and exactly what they said. An opinion would fall along the lines of commentary stating that it was a terrible speech.

This skill seems especially important for Christians to work on as part of our fact-checking world. As we engage with people and news in online spaces, how can we practice recognizing the difference between fact and opinion? If we want to be loving in our online spaces or having kind conversations with our neighbors, how can we practice expressing opinions that are based in facts?

REFLECTION QUESTIONS

- When is the last time you paused when reading the news to notice whether someone reported fact or opinion?
- When you notice your emotions online, have you paused to notice whether you respond emotionally to factual statements or opinions?

EXERCISE 5.6: FACTS AND OPINIONS

Taking the time to notice whether what you see online is fact or opinion can make you a much wiser consumer of information.

People often get overly emotional about things they see online that are opinions, not facts. Although this may feel elementary to you, it's always worth taking on the role of a learner and checking in with our own knowledge.

STEP 1. Find a news story about a current event.

STEP 2. Read through and see if you can identify the facts (who, what, where, when) and the opinions (judgments, interpretations, etc.). Go line by line. If it's a print news story, try circling the facts and underlining the opinions.

STEP 3. Reflect on the experience of identifying both types of statements. Was it easy? Was it hard? If it was difficult, consider having someone else read the story, too, and talk about what you both identified. Reflect on how practicing this skill makes you more able to engage with information wisely.

ONE FINAL FRAMEWORK

Before we wrap up this conversation around tools, techniques, and practices for fact-checking, I want to share one last framework that may be helpful for you. It summarizes a lot of what we've talked about both in this chapter and the previous one. Several years ago, librarians at Pennsylvania State University Libraries developed a framework called IF I APPLY, which walks us through steps for evaluating information. This framework covers all the things we've talked about in this chapter, and I include it for those of you that find this type of acronym helpful. We all remember new things differently, so if this framework is helpful for you, great! If not, that's okay too.

This framework starts with some personal steps you can take before evaluating information. It then includes the steps you can take to actually evaluate a piece of information:

Personal Steps:

I—Identify emotions attached to topic.

F—Find unbiased reference sources for proper review of topic.

I—Intellectual courage to seek authoritative voices on topic that may be outside of [our comfort zone].

Source steps:

A—Authority established. Does the author have education and experience in that field?

P—Purpose/Point of view of source. Does the author have an agenda beyond education or information?

P—Publisher. Does the publisher have an agenda?

L—List of sources (bibliography).

Y—Year of publication.[8]

What I find so compelling about these steps is that they, too, start with us. Yes, we should care about publishers' agendas and whether the creator has the education necessary to be an expert. But so much of our fact-checking work starts with us—knowing our emotions, which we talked about in the previous chapter, and knowing our own biases. We'll be much more effective with the source steps listed if we've taken the time to engage with the personal steps first. It reminds me a bit of Matthew 7:3–5, which reminds us to take the plank out of our own eye before removing the speck from our brother's. Sometimes we need to look inward before we can look outward.

WRAPPING UP

Whew! We've covered a lot! I know this chapter includes a lot of very practical tools and advice along with some more personal practices, which can be a bit overwhelming. But all these skills and tools are the key to being wise in our online spaces. They're the practices where the rubber meets the road, so to say. Just like our faith has regular spiritual practices that give us grounding and help us actually grow in the ways we want to grow, these tools and practices of evaluating information help us grow in how we engage with information. None of the things mentioned in this chapter come easy to us; they take practice and time.

But if we want to continue to press into being truth-seekers, we need to practice these things. Each of these tools will give you a few steps to help you find truth around you, truth in current events, and truth in social issues.

REFLECTION QUESTIONS

- What do you find most challenging about these concepts?
- How can you invite the Holy Spirit into these practices?
- Can you identify your own motivation for wanting to try these fact-checking tips? Connecting hard things to our motivation will help us stick with it when it's hard.
- Of all the tools and practices mentioned in this chapter, which ones feel the hardest to try? Which do you want to start with?

ADDITIONAL RESOURCES

Ad Fontes Media Bias Chart. https://adfontesmedia.com/. This website provides a chart like the one shown in this chapter from AllSides.com. This one is regularly updated and includes a wide variety of media, from news outlets to podcasts. Keep in mind that this is a helpful tool for us to reflect on our own media consumption. If you find all your news sources fall within one area, consider engaging with a new media outlet.

AllSides.com. https://www.allsides.com/. This website includes a number of helpful tools. You can see headlines of current events from different perspectives side by side in order to get a fuller picture of what's happening around the world. They've also created the chart shown in this chapter that can help you reflect on the different places you get your news and information from. Remember, a bias chart isn't meant to imply that sources with bias are all bad but that we can build awareness around what bias might be present in the news we consume. Use the tools on this website for self-reflection.

Caulfield, Mike. *Web Literacy for Student Fact-Checkers*. Self-published, 2017. https://webliteracy.pressbooks.com/. This free ebook was originally written for college students but has many examples of how to fact-check using the tools from this chapter. Most examples are prepandemic and focus on social media. But it may be helpful to see other examples of the tools and skills discussed in this chapter. Caulfield has since changed his framework slightly, but this book is a great starting place for learning these tools.

Checkology. https://get.checkology.org/. A free, online course created by News Literacy Project. Created for educators but available to the public, this website includes several free lessons to help you become more news literate, including many ways to fact-check what you see online.

CTRL-F. https://m.youtube.com/c/CTRLF. This YouTube channel includes videos on many different online skills. In particular, they include a series of videos on fact-checking techniques, also by Mike Caulfield. If you're a visual or auditory learner, these videos can be helpful for seeing real-life examples of fact-checking. Note that these examples, in contrast to the ones in his ebook, are newer and may cover more current events. He has also updated his framework from Four Moves and Habit to the acronym SIFT; although the specific tools are the same, they may appear under different names.

"Fake News: How to Spot Misinformation." In NPR's *Life Kit*. Podcast audio. October 31, 2019. https://www.npr.org/2019/10/29/774541010/fake-news-is-scary-heres-how-to-spot-misinformation. This podcast has many of the same fact-checking tips recommended in this book, from checking emotions to understanding the information landscape. It may be helpful to hear some of these tips in podcast form if you're an auditory learner.

Harvard Implicit Bias Test. https://implicit.harvard.edu/implicit
/takeatest.html. A regularly recommended online resource to
help reveal and reflect on your implicit biases. Use this test to help
you think about the areas in which you may have bias in how you
look at the world. Then reflect on how those biases may impact
the type of information you choose to engage with (or not!).

Otis, Cindy L. *True or False: A CIA Analyst's Guide to Spotting Fake
News.* New York: Feiwel and Friends, 2020. This book is mentioned in an earlier chapter as a resource because it both gives an
overview of the history of fake news and contains a number of
different and helpful techniques to help you spot misinformation.
Some of the techniques are the same as the ones we discussed
here, but there are some additional, helpful tools.

Deciding What to Do

Once we understand the information landscape and have evaluated what we see and hear, we're on to step 3 of the framework for consuming information wisely. One last time, here's that framework:

1. Understand the information landscape.
2. Evaluate the information you find, see, read, or hear.
3. Choose and discern how you want to engage with the information, including:
   a. loving your (online) neighbors and speaking truth to other people and those who believe misinformation
   b. practicing humility in learning new perspectives.

We can and do regularly make choices about how we want to engage with information. One of the main goals of this book is to avoid being complacent or passive when it comes to this last step of the framework. It's easy to sit back, watch our streaming videos, read some news, scroll through social media, and never take stock of our reactions or notice how we respond, either internally or externally. As Christians, we want to keep our focus on being intentional and loving and speaking truth.

This last section helps us take what we've learned and apply it to ourselves and our conversations.

As we engage with the process of fact-checking and digging deeper on issues, we can look for productive ways to respond, both internally and externally. This is yet another place where we can ask the Holy Spirit for wisdom and guidance. As I've been working with different churches, from different denominations, around these concepts, two things keep coming up in this last step of engagement: first, how important it is for us to engage with different perspectives and, second, to practice talking with people with whom we disagree by loving our online neighbors well. Because I see the same things come up regardless of which church I've worked with, it makes me think that these are things people all across the church struggle with. This last section of the book will focus on both of these practices as we take all we've learned about fact-checking and the information landscape and apply it to our relationships.

As we've moved through the different aspects of being wise in our online spaces, we've talked in chapters 1–3 about understanding the big picture—learning more about the information landscape—as the first step. And we've talked in chapters 4–5 about how to evaluate information—different ways to think critically and fact-check. We're now on our final step and section and can think about what to do with the information we engage with. How do we want to respond to what we see, listen to, and read online?

CHAPTER 6

Purposefully Seeking Out
New Perspectives

A couple of years ago, a former colleague of mine reached out when he heard about the classes I gave at churches. He said he appreciated what I did to help Christians discern truth in their online spaces, as he'd been discouraged by some of what he saw around him and how many Christians weren't seeking truth but falling victim to conspiracy theories. Soon after, he sent me this excerpt from Howard Thurman's book *Meditations of the Heart*, because he said it reminded him of my work. Howard Thurman was a theologian and civil rights leader. He was also the dean of the chapel at Howard University and then later at Boston University in the mid-twentieth century. The excerpt my colleague sent me was this:

> I will keep my heart open this day to all things that commend themselves to me as truth. I will try to increase my sensitivity to error that it may not enter my heart with its distortions and its falseness. This is not easy. I am never free from the possibility of being mistaken. Deep within myself I will be still, that I may be guided and wisened by the Spirit of God. In

my own way, I will work out little tests by which I may discern truth from error. Error may enter my mind and heart in many disguises, this I know. My anxieties, my fears, my ambitions, even my hopes and my dreams may deceive me into calling truth, error; and error, truth. Always I will seek the honesty and integrity that God yields to those who lay bare their lives constantly before him.[1]

I've read this short excerpt multiple times since then and often share it in the classes I teach as a reminder that false information or error can enter our hearts and minds more easily than we might like to admit. In our current internet culture, false information is everywhere. I find it fascinating that he wrote this in 1953, long before our current internet culture. It's such a great reminder that as people of faith, we stand on the shoulders of those who came before us, and many of them, too, were struggling with some of the same things we also battle. They, too, sought ways to find truth in their own contexts. Human beings have always been susceptible to false information, and Christians are no exception. Thurman mentions little tests. I don't know what his little tests were to help him find the truth, but in today's culture, some of our tests might be ones we've been talking about in this book, as we fact-check and check our emotions and try to discern truth in our online spaces. What tests do you currently use? Ultimately, though, what I hope we can realize is that we're "never free from the possibility of being mistaken."

There's also room for us to pay attention to the role of humility in this work. What I mean is this: How can we engage with information in a way that helps us grow and think outside our opinions or, as Thurman says, notice whether we're mistaken? I'm not saying we should automatically think we're mistaken and I'm also not saying we need to change our opinions on everything. But is it possible that we could practice some humility and engage with others in a more curious and open-minded way? Are we able to value the opinions of others who have a perspective different from ours? And can we appreciate someone who has a different value system? We may be prone to end dialogue with others when our values clash, we may dehumanize those with whom we disagree by othering them—assuming they're in a group different from us. But I hope that we can notice when we might be mistaken and practice humility as we engage with new perspectives.

PRACTICING HUMILITY

Humility isn't a new concept for those of us with Christian faith. We read about it in the Bible and talk about it at church. And once again, as Christ-followers, we have an opportunity to be different in all our spaces, both physical and online—acting differently and speaking differently. *Merriam-Webster* defines "humble" as "not proud or haughty" or "not arrogant."[2] These are qualities that many Christians—probably you, too!—want to have in their lives. We talk about practicing humility quite a bit as Christians. But what does humility look like when we engage with information and social media and current events and news?

If I'm honest, I don't always practice humility when engaging online, especially when it comes to not being prideful or arrogant or not thinking of myself as better than others. I'm just as guilty as anyone else of seeing what someone posts online and rolling my eyes, judging them, and feeling superior because I know better about X, Y, and Z topics. Again, I'm not saying I can't have a different opinion about those topics, but my dismissive and superior attitude isn't exactly practicing humility. I might even be right about a particular topic, but that doesn't mean I need to think of myself as better or smarter than someone else. And some topics don't even have a right or wrong, just a different perspective rooted in individual values. Based on the conversations I've had with others in my classes, I suspect I'm not the only one that struggles with this.

And in addition to the dictionary definition of humility, we know there are lots of Bible passages that talk about humility, such as the following:

- Proverbs 11:2: "When pride comes, then comes disgrace, but with humility comes wisdom" (NIV).
- Colossians 3:12: "Therefore, as God's chosen people, holy and dearly loved, clothe yourselves with compassion, kindness, humility, gentleness and patience" (NIV).
- Luke 14:11: "For all those who exalt themselves will be humbled, and those who humble themselves will be exalted" (NIV).
- Micah 6:8: "He has shown you, O mortal, what is good. And what does the Lord require of you? To act justly and to love mercy and to walk humbly with your God" (NIV).

And this is only a sampling of passages reminding us that humility is something God talks about, as a fruit of the Spirit. If we come from a Christian background, we've likely heard this concept talked about in church, or we've talked about these passages or similar ones. And while I like the dictionary definition of not thinking we're better than others, it's helpful to remind ourselves that this is also a virtue that's important to many within the church.

Please know that I don't think practicing humility means we can't or shouldn't disagree with others. Nor does it mean that we can't or shouldn't speak up against misinformation and conspiracy theories. But rather, the posture of our heart is one that doesn't assume we're superior to others. Reflecting on our heart posture may be a better starting point for those conversations in which we disagree with someone or need to confront someone about misinformation.

Ultimately, this step of humility and our responses to others are ones we discuss quite a bit in my classes, because, again, it seems like a logical place for people of faith to act differently than the rest of the world, to be the salt and light Jesus talks about in Matthew 5. Think for a minute about how you see people respond in your online spaces (social media, reading news, etc.). Do you see people do any of the following things? Or, if you're willing to dig a bit deeper and be vulnerable, have you ever done any of these things yourself?

- Left rude comments on news stories and social media posts?
- Responded to someone online instead of having what might have been a more productive in-person conversation?
- Shared a post quickly, without context, in a way that implies there wasn't much fact-checking done before sharing?
- Used language that implied an us-versus-them mentality, creating black-and-white sides in an issue?
- Judged or shamed someone solely based on something they've posted online?

The list could go on. We see these things all the time in our online spaces, and sometimes they bleed into our real-world conversations. And we might be guilty of doing some of these things ourselves—responding out of anger or fear, sharing without double-checking, thinking we're right on an issue without actually listening to another perspective. These are real responses. I'm guilty of some of them myself. If we're not careful, these responses can become habits that also form us in ways that aren't Christlike. I know I don't always practice a posture of listening or reading for understanding, or even humility, but assume they're wrong and I'm right. I've definitely responded in prideful ways, even if they were just internal responses. Take a minute and write down any responses you'd add to this list. In which ones do you practice humility, and in which ones do you try to be right or prove a point?

So, what does this humility actually look like? What does it look like to increase our sensitivity to error? It looks like many of the things we've already talked about in previous chapters: checking our emotions, fact-checking outrageous claims, noticing our bias, reading different perspectives. All the things we've described so far help you lead a life of understanding the online world and engaging in a way that hopefully helps you not think of yourself as better than others.

Christians want to be truth-tellers. We want to share the truth and peace we have in knowing Jesus, but sometimes I wonder whether that might lead us to be a bit too arrogant, insisting we have the truth around a social issue or current event before we've even had a chance to listen to the other side(s), or before we've even examined the issue in light of our faith, or before we've looked at multiple sources about the issue. Our faith might grow if we're willing to listen and understand other perspectives before offering our own solutions or opinions.

A lack of humility might also look like judging the people around us based solely on their chosen news sources. A church leader recently described it to me, as people were reading different news sources and not only judging others for reading fill-in-the-blank news sources but also assuming that if someone read certain news sources, their faith was somehow lacking. This church leader observed that those in the congregation weren't practicing humility and were actually being quite judgmental toward each other. This was convicting for me too. How often do I not only judge someone for their choice of news or information but also judge their faith because of it? I was reminded in that conversation that everyone is made in the image of God, even the people who read news sources different from those I do. But that's very hard to remember sometimes! That church leader also noticed that it was making it difficult for people to sit across the aisle from people in the church because they were getting so focused on who was right about the news instead of seeing each other as part of the body of Christ.

I feel the need to pause here and say again, I'm not talking about letting people believe misinformation or dangerous false information or conspiracy theories. We'll talk in the next chapter about what it means to love others well and to talk with them about those things, which are equally important. People sometimes think I mean that we need to practice humility to the point of being quiet or passive or let others believe conspiracy theories. I'm not. Instead, I believe that in order for us to speak up against misinformation, we need to do some self-reflection and notice our own hearts first so that we're better prepared for those conversations. As with checking our emotions, it's helpful to pause before reacting, to center ourselves before we act on misinformation. However, I know that can be hard to do in the middle of a conversation.

For example, maybe you attend a family gathering and you hear a relative say something you believe to be misinformation. How do you respond? I suspect there are a range of options we might choose:

- either respond quickly, telling the person they're wrong and giving your own information
- take a deep breath and ask them where they got their information
- practice curiosity and listen to their views, knowing it will help you understand them better
- or start a debate on the issue, enlisting others to join you.

These varied responses to our loved ones—and I'm sure there are others—can also create a variety of situations in our relationships and ourselves. Some will result in more humility for ourselves; others will result in more division in our relationships. Which do you lean toward? Consider reflecting on how your response to someone might allow you to practice humility more than proving a point.

HOLDING THE TENSION

As we incorporate humility into our online practices, there are a few helpful things to keep in mind. There are many truths in the Bible that we can look to, and it helps to remember that the books of the Bible were written for specific groups of people at specific times in history. It doesn't address many of our current issues and events directly—a global pandemic, racial unrest and tension, vaccines, and so on. The pastor of a church I worked with once said during one of my sessions, "The Bible might not say anything directly about taking the COVID vaccine, but it does have something to say about loving our neighbors," which I thought was a helpful way of looking at the current pandemic and vaccine conversations we saw in the news. It was a reminder to look at the messages we see in Scripture—to take what we know about Jesus and the Bible as a whole—and apply them as best we can to our current circumstances.

But that might not always mean we know best or are right on every topic. If we believe that all truth is God's truth, what would it look like to both seek truth online (fact-check and dig deeper) and rely on the Holy Spirit and Scripture to reveal truth to us in new ways as we engage with our online spaces?

Sometimes we can get caught up in either-or thinking in our online spaces. Either we fact-check everything, looking for the logical and scientific view and answers. Or we say, "God will prompt me on what to research, and his word, the Bible, is the only truth I need; I won't worry about anything else." But what if we need both our faith and our logic? There's space for us to listen to the Holy Spirit and continue fact-checking and investigating current issues.

In a Faith and Fake News class, someone once started a question with "Apparently, we're supposed to believe in science now" and then proceeded to ask a question about the news. I was so surprised by his statement I almost didn't know what to say. My impression was that he pitted science against his faith as he asked a question about the online environment. But what if there's room to hold both science and faith? Truth that comes from fact-checking and scriptural truth? What if we can use both our faith and our critical thinking skills to learn more about the world around us, the world God created and loves?

Can you identify any areas in your life in which you've fallen into either-or thinking about faith and fact-checking? I once got an email from a Faith and Fake News–class participant several months after the class concluded. She thanked me again for offering the class and said how she found it so helpful. She also said she doesn't always fact-check everything the way I taught (using the skills in chapter 4) but that she always pauses and asks the Holy Spirit for wisdom. On the one hand, I thought, "Great, at least she's pausing and paying attention online!" On the other hand, I couldn't quite tell whether she relied solely on the Holy Spirit to prompt her on whether something was true and skipped any fact-checking skills altogether.

Maybe you're tempted to do the same—to rely on either your spiritual intuition or your rational brain. Both are important. And both have value. We can learn to hold the tension between our faith and what we see.

In another class, a participant brought up another helpful point about humility and either-or thinking. She reminded us all that when Jesus interacted with people, he didn't rush. And even more importantly, he also often responded to questions with more questions or open-ended responses, or both. Although he was the ultimate truth-teller, he didn't always give people straight answers (much to their frustration, I imagine) but responded with open-ended prompts; his questions and responses allowed him to find his intersection with the culture at the time and ultimately teach them other ways to think about issues. This is another way we can practice humility with those around us. Instead of rushing to answer someone's question or comment with a "here's exactly what you need to know or do" response, what would it look like if we responded with openness and curiosity and questions?

WHICH LENS DO YOU LOOK THROUGH?

In his book *Thou Shalt Not Be a Jerk*, Eugene Cho posits that many Christians in the United States have taken their political views and put them in front of their theology or faith. That is to say, for many Christians, we look at our faith through the lens of our political perspective instead of letting our politics be informed by the lens of our faith. "From a political perspective, cultural Christianity is when our theology is held captive by our politics rather than our politics being informed and even transformed by our theology."[3] While I generally don't talk about politics in this book or in my classes, I do see many parallels between what Cho says about our politics and how we approach information, because so much information we consume is political. How often do we approach our news consumption through our political or ideological lenses first, and then our theological ones?

What I mean is this: Do we approach the information we consume online, in the news and on social media from our political lenses first? Do we interpret what we see and read based on our politics? Or do we approach the information we consume from our faith? Do we look at the world to engage with it the way Jesus did, by loving the marginalized and caring for the sick, looking after the widows and the orphans?

I suspect we don't always do that. I admit I sometimes just seek out the information that backs my opinion and ideas, without thinking about whether I'm looking at the issue through my faith and what Jesus would want. In the United States especially, there's a lot of partisan, political language in the information we consume and how we talk about social issues. It's not hard to interpret information through those views. But I love how Cho encourages us to seek first the kingdom of God and then look at the world. The same can be said about how we consume information, read the news, and talk about current events. We can approach these venues with Jesus's heart first to help us interpret what we see and hear.

For example, as I write this, current world events are centered around eastern Europe. Russia's military has recently invaded neighboring Ukraine, causing mass destruction. Millions of refugees seek safety in neighboring countries, and the news is full of images of bombed-out buildings and people fleeing. I have a choice when I consume news about events like this. I can either approach the images and social media feeds with the mind of Christ first—one of love and compassion for the brokenhearted—and then interpret what I see, deciding how to respond. This is what Cho calls us to do. Or I can approach what I see by thinking, "How does my political party respond to this crisis?" and let that impact the way I respond. Do you see the difference? We can take the mind of Christ into these online spaces, allowing him to help us determine our next steps in interpreting and responding.

FINDING NEW PERSPECTIVES

In the previous chapter, we talked about news bias and different places to get your news. We talked about media bias charts as a way to think about the different places we get our news from and the importance of reading news from multiple sources to get a fuller picture of the news. In addition to getting a more complete picture of world events, reading multiple news sources is also a helpful way to examine our willingness to practice humility. Are you willing to read different news sources? Not with the intention of pointing out their flaws but out of a sense of curiosity? With a posture of humility that you might have something else to learn? Full disclosure: I admit, this is another thing I find incredibly difficult. It's not hard for me to check out a news source different from my usual sources, but I generally lean toward a posture of judgment when I look at them. I think, "Wow, people read this and believe it?" I don't approach this exercise with curiosity every time.

I'm not saying you have to engage with different news sources and immediately change your mind on a social or political issue. But the reality is, if we can practice humility and curiosity, we might learn something new. You may try different spiritual practices to help you develop these skills, such as prayer, serving others, and regular reflection on the Bible. Note that in this case, I also mean news sources that have proven to be trustworthy and are reputable, not ones that are known for sharing conspiracy theories. We don't need to read bad news sources to widen our perspective. If you're not sure whether a news source is trustworthy, go back to the section on lateral reading in the previous chapter or look at one of the media bias charts to give you some more information.

I also don't want to imply that there's no truth in our world. Christians in general agree on certain truths from Scripture, such as Jesus as Savior or that God loves us. But there are so many things never mentioned in Scripture, and we have to take what we know of the overall story of God presented in Scripture and apply it to the information we consume. Admittedly, this can be confusing, as so many different church denominations have come to different conclusions about a myriad of topics. But it's worth acknowledging that the overall narrative of Scripture doesn't always address specific issues we face today.

Reading multiple news sources can also help us practice what psychologist Adam Grant calls "thinking again." In his book *Think Again: The Power of Knowing What You Don't Know*, Grant lays out the importance of "unknowing." He talks about being curious and thinking like a scientist. Scientists test hypotheses and keep trying new things to learn more about the world. (Remember the scientific process we talked about in chapter 2?) What would it look like for us to adopt a similar way of life, testing hypothesis after hypothesis, continually trying out new things and testing what we think we know about a topic?

Grant doesn't say that we shouldn't have convictions or that we can't have specific beliefs about things, like religion or faith. But what does it look like to be willing to test what we think we know about the world, ourselves, or other people before jumping to conclusions? Can we make sense of a situation after we've gathered all the information? Grant puts it this way:

> Great thinkers don't harbor doubts because they're imposters. They maintain doubts because they know we're all partially blind and they're committed to improving their sight. They don't boast about how much they know; they marvel at how little they understand. They're aware that each answer raises new questions, and the quest for knowledge is never finished. A mark of lifelong learners is recognizing that they can learn something from everyone they meet. Arrogance leaves us blind to our weaknesses. Humility is a reflective lens: it helps us see them clearly. Confident humility is a corrective lens: it enables us to overcome those weaknesses.[4]

We grow as human beings when we question the world around us, when we're willing to look a bit deeper and at the nuance of a situation. This involves a level of curiosity for ourselves and the world around us. If we want to find new perspectives and be willing to find the nuances of a situation, we need to practice curiosity. Being curious is part of the scientist way of thinking that Grant talks about.

So, what's an example of getting outside our own (filter) bubble? How can we recognize that we might need to get outside our own spaces and listen to someone else? Here's one recent example from my own life. I live in Minneapolis, Minnesota, which has been at the center of a lot of current conversations around police reform in the United States, after the killing of George Floyd in 2020 by police officer Derek Chauvin. In 2021, Minneapolis residents voted on a few local races and issues, including whether to replace the Minneapolis Police Department with a Department of Public Safety. Like any good citizen, I read different viewpoints and cast my vote the way I felt fit my values. Once all the votes were counted, the proposal didn't pass, and I was very surprised. I quickly realized that my surprise came not necessarily from how I voted but from how small my information bubbles were. The news I had consumed and the people I had followed and talked with discussed the measure as if it were a done deal and would pass without a problem. But clearly it didn't.

Anytime we're surprised by something we assumed would happen—or didn't happen—it's worth examining our filter bubbles a bit more. Do we engage with only one kind of news source? Do all the people in our circles (online or in person) think one way on a topic? I'm not even saying we have to agree with the outcome or the assumed conclusion. I'm focusing more on the surprise we feel; one way or another, it could be an indication that we live in a bubble, either online or in person. If we're curious about and reflect on why we're surprised, we might learn something about ourselves and our own views or how we interact with information and others.

Take a minute and write down some of the filter bubbles you see in your life. We talked about this earlier in the book, but it's helpful to reflect again now that we're exploring this idea of humility and curiosity. Can you identify any bubbles you might be in, whether they're from your news sources or the people around you?

Being open-minded and humble doesn't mean we have to agree with everything someone says, but it's closely related to listening well and being curious about someone else's conclusions. And again, we don't need to let them believe false information, but there's an important step here for us to reflect on our own responses. It's worth reflecting on whether we need to start with ourselves before we try to change someone's mind on false information or other issues.

In a class I was giving a couple of years ago, I mentioned that being willing to engage with different perspectives allowed us to find the gray spaces of current events. Reading multiple news stories with different perspectives might help us find the gray of a situation instead of focusing on the black or white. (Remember how online spaces are designed to be emotional? Part of that is showing only one side of an issue.) While I was talking about finding nuance in current events and holding the tension of multiple sides, someone interrupted me and said, "Wait, did you say gray spaces or grace spaces?" I explained that I said gray but that actually grace spaces were also something for us to consider. In fact, the next chapter will focus specifically on how we can love our neighbors better, including our online neighbors, which is exactly where those grace spaces exist.

REFLECTION QUESTIONS

- When was the last time you read a news source different from your usual source with the intention of simply trying to learn? (Not to be annoyed and frustrated and prove your source or view is better or right.)
- When was the last time you had a conversation with someone who thought differently than you on a social issue with the intention to simply listen?
- When was the last time you were willing to say, "I don't know"? Were you willing to say you don't know about a social issue? What about an issue relating to your faith?

- Reflect on Howard Thurman's meditation: What kind of regular reflection might you incorporate into your life so that you can recognize the times when you aren't free of the possibility of being wrong?
- Do you get your news from a variety of sources in order to better understand all sides of an issue? (See exercise 6.1 to help you think about finding new perspectives.)
- When was the last time you changed an opinion or view? When was the last time you admitted you were wrong—even if only to yourself? What was it about?

EXERCISE 6.1: SEEKING NEW PERSPECTIVES

In this chapter, we talked about the importance of seeking out different perspectives and practicing humility, recognizing that we may need to learn more about a particular topic. Use this exercise to reflect on the types of news and information sources you regularly seek out—and how to include some new ones. By seeking out new news and information sources, you'll become more well-rounded on the topics that are important to you.

STEP 1. List all the ways you currently get your news or information about a topic that's important to you. This can be specific news websites (i.e., BBC News) and platforms you rely on (e.g., Facebook).

STEP 2. Go to a media bias chart—either from AllSides.com or from Ad Fontes Media. You can find a version in chapter 5 or look them up online.

STEP 3. Look at where your current news sources fall on the chart, and reflect on the following questions:

- Do all your news sources fall in one area of the chart?
- Do they cover a range of space on the chart?
- Why are you drawn to the sources you currently read or watch?
- If you objectively look at some of your regular news sources, do you notice any bias in them?

STEP 4. Identify one news source on the chart (or ask a friend who has views different from yours where they get their news) that you want to read or follow for a time. Remember that bias that's present in some news sources doesn't necessarily mean the source has inaccurate reporting.

STEP 5. Read or watch the news from the new source every day for five days. You may choose to engage with the new source in addition to or instead of your current sources. Note that you don't necessarily need to increase the time you spend on the news; just focus that time on a different source.

STEP 6. Reflect on the following questions: What do you notice about how you view current events? Did you notice different types of stories or issues being highlighted? What did you learn? Did you change your mind about anything? Did you notice news stories with more or less facts or opinions or rereporting? Spend some time reflecting or praying about what you notice. Where might the Spirit be leading you?

EXERCISE 6.2: THURMAN MEDITATION

Reread the meditation by Howard Thurman on pages 129–30. Use these questions to reflect on the passage:

- What tests do you use to discern truth from error? What do those tests look like in your spiritual life compared to how you look at information? Given what you've learned so far in this book, do any of those tests need to change?

- What spiritual or other practices do you have in place to help you discern truth from error and error from truth?
- When have you let error into your mind or heart? How did you know?

EXERCISE 6.3: IDENTIFYING THE LENSES YOU LOOK THROUGH

As we think about engaging with different perspectives, it's helpful to identify the different lenses we look through when we engage with political views, current events, the news, and so on. These different lenses are the ways in which we see the world. We likely look through different ones at different times or with different information. Use this exercise to reflect on the lenses you see the world through and which ones you use at different times.

STEP 1. Write down a list of the different identities you might look at the world through. For example, I might list these: Christian, librarian, American, female, and so on. Write down the characteristics of each.

STEP 2. The next time you engage with the news or some other piece of information, notice which identity or lens you use to interpret the information. This takes an incredible amount of self-awareness and practice. Do you react out of the fact that you're a Christian? Out of your political views? Something else?

STEP 3. Reflect on how you interpret the news. What do you notice about the lenses or identities you use? How might they be different from the ones others around you use?

ADDITIONAL RESOURCES

"Changing Our Minds." In *TED Radio Hour*. Podcast audio. December 3, 2021. https://www.npr.org/programs/ted-radio-hour/1056 207681/changing-our-minds? This podcast episode features three different TED speakers that help us think about what it looks like to practice humility and change our minds about people and issues. The speakers come from a range of perspectives themselves, which I find helpful. Sometimes hearing someone else's story can help us reflect on our own.

Cho, Eugene. *Thou Shalt Not Be a Jerk*. Colorado Springs: David C. Cook, 2020. This book helps readers move beyond partisan thinking and evaluate whether their politics takes a more prominent role in their views than the gospel itself does. Although I generally don't talk about politics per se in this book, there are some helpful things that we can reflect on.

The Flip Side. https://www.theflipside.io/. Sign up for a daily email summarizing a current topic with viewpoints from multiple sides of the political spectrum, with the goal of seeing different arguments on the same issue. The nice thing about this is that it'll come straight to your inbox!

Grant, Adam, *Think Again: The Power of Knowing What You Don't Know*. New York: Viking, 2021. This book helps us think through what it looks like to stay curious about our world and be willing to be wrong. Grant focuses a lot on thinking like a scientist—being willing to question the way we look at the world and to test our own hypotheses.

———. "What Frogs in Hot Water Can Teach Us about Thinking Again." TED video. April 2021. https://www.ted.com/talks/adam_grant _what_frogs_in_hot_water_can_teach_us_about_thinking_again ?language=en. A summary of many of the concepts in his book *Think Again*, including the concept of confident humility, which Grant describes as "being secure enough in your strengths to acknowledge your weaknesses." If you don't have time to read the whole book, at least consider watching this TED talk.

O'Brien, Stephanie Williams. *Stay Curious: How Questions and Doubts Can Save Your Faith*. Minneapolis: Fortress, 2019. While this book focuses a lot on how living a life of curiosity can help your faith, there are some helpful reflections here that are relevant to our online spaces. O'Brien's work is a helpful guide for us as Christians to explore what it means to experience doubt and questions and still stay connected to our faith.

CHAPTER 7

Loving Our Neighbors

When I offered my first Faith and Fake News class in early 2020, I thought I'd primarily teach practical tools to the participants. I approached that very first six-week class the way I approach my classes as an academic librarian: very structured and full of fact-checking, information evaluation tools. I approached it in the way I was trained professionally: to create lesson plans with learning outcomes. But it became obvious to me within the first class that while people wanted tools to know what was true online and what wasn't, they were equally looking for tools to know how to talk with their friends and family about current events.

So I did another thing I was trained to do: I pivoted to help meet the needs of the people in the class. I still taught them fact-checking tools, but I made sure to add content around relationships and leave space for people to process what they saw in their contexts in terms of talking with people they cared about. We spent a lot of time discussing people's personal experiences, both with their online environments and their loved ones. This is a change I've kept throughout all the classes since: space for discussion and reflection around talking with others.

This last chapter represents a lot of conversations in a lot of classes over the last few years. It represents a part of faith and fake news I didn't expect to be as important as it is. But in retrospect, it makes perfect sense and is the crux of all of the fact-checking and information seeking we do. It's the conclusion of all the conversations around fact-checking. It's why we engage with these practices and tools. It was the relational pieces that led me to want to offer the class to begin with—all those conversations with friends saying they weren't sure how to talk with their friends and family about current events. So, as we head toward the end of this book, this chapter is about how we practice kindness and love our neighbors both in our online spaces and in using the information we find online.

LOVING OUR NEIGHBORS

Throughout the conversations I've engaged in around this work, I keep coming back to the core Christian value of loving our neighbors. Not only are we called to be people of truth, but Jesus also tells us to love the people around us. One of our goals as we fact-check isn't only to seek truth but also to find ways to love others through what we find. There are a number of places we could start a conversation about being kind and loving our online neighbors, but I like to start with these famous verses from Mark 12:30–31:

> ³⁰"'Love the Lord your God with all your heart and with all your soul and with all your mind and with all your strength.'
> ³¹The second is this: 'Love your neighbor as yourself.' There is no commandment greater than these." (NIV)

These verses in Mark are Jesus's response to a teacher of the law asking what the most important commandment is. They're often quoted in the church, and those of us who grew up in Christian faith communities probably heard them applied in all kinds of contexts, from loving our physical next-door neighbors to supporting missionaries around the world.

But because this commandment is from a different time in history, I can't help but reflect on how different our neighbors are now compared to when Jesus spoke these words. When Jesus lived, the concept of neighbor must have been so different. Could that religious teacher of the law or the disciples imagine a world where we can chat with people hundreds of miles away, whether via phone, video, or social media? Who are our neighbors in this hyperconnected, online world? This is something I keep coming back to when talking about these concepts; if our world and culture are increasingly online, we need to know how to love our online neighbors just as much as we learn to love our in-person neighbors.

Or if you've grown up in a Christian tradition, you've likely also heard the parable of the good Samaritan from Luke 10:

> [25]On one occasion an expert in the law stood up to test Jesus. "Teacher," he asked, "what must I do to inherit eternal life?" [26]"What is written in the Law?" he replied. "How do you read it?" [27]He answered, "'Love the Lord your God with all your heart and with all your soul and with all your strength and with all your mind'; and, 'Love your neighbor as yourself.'" [28]"You have answered correctly," Jesus replied. "Do this and you will live." [29]But he wanted to justify himself, so he asked Jesus, "And who is my neighbor?" (NIV)

And instead of answering the expert in the law directly about who is his neighbor, Jesus replies with the parable or story of the good Samaritan. A man is attacked by robbers, and none of the people you'd expect to help him do. Instead, it's the Samaritan, hated by the Jewish people, who has mercy on the man who was attacked. This story is one many of us who have grown up in

Christian settings have heard many times; it can be easy to nod along. And like the verses in Mark, this story was written at a specific time in history to a specific group of people. But what might it have to say to us living in a hyperconnected world, full of videos and news and social media? Who are our neighbors today? Who are the unexpected neighbors we might be called to care about?

Again, not to overspiritualize, but in light of these two passages, who are our neighbors in our current culture? Who are the people we pass by? Who are the people in our culture that are like the good Samaritan? The ones we wouldn't expect to provide help? Can we be that person, that good neighbor, to someone else? I can't help but wonder what our online spaces would look like if we chose to purposely look out for people or situations of suffering online and speak truth about injustice.

There are plenty of other Bible passages we could look at, but both of these help us start to recenter ourselves on what Jesus commands us to do with regard to caring about other people. Both passages refer to loving our neighbors, and we need to think about who our neighbors are when we live so much of our lives online. After all that technical information in this book about the information landscape and all those practical fact-checking tools, it comes down to this: What will we do when we seek and find the truth of a situation online? How will we love our neighbors in our online spaces? How will we respond to what we see online, and how will it impact those around us? Yes, it's great if we can learn more about current events and the truth of what's happening in the world. But if we don't take that knowledge and find ways to engage with others kindly and productively and, yes, even lovingly, we fall short of loving our neighbors well.

And like the good Samaritan, can we look past someone's background or what society expects of us and love them anyway? I often bring this up in the workshops I teach: What does it look like for you to hold someone's humanity as they're made

in the image of God but not hold the potentially false information they believe? Or at least to be willing to love them if they
get their information from somewhere other than where you
get yours? Inevitably, this question sparks a lot of conversation
around what it means to separate people from the information
they believe. And usually we can all admit that it's hard to do!

ONLINE NEIGHBORS

As we think about loving others and focusing on relationships,
we also need to think about all the spaces in which our relationships occur. Thinking back to the two scriptures at the beginning
of this chapter, our neighbors are, yes, the people we encounter every day at work and at home. But as more of our time is
spent online and on social media, we can also think about who
are our neighbors in those spaces as well. In some ways, I sup-
pose our online neighbors fall into the same or similar categories
as our real-world neighbors, for example:

- acquaintances—those we say hello to but have trouble remembering their names (these might be the "you may know" list of
  people on social media)
- people you invite over for a backyard barbecue or fire and have
  long conversations with about real life—the ones you might
  send DMs to on social media or ask to borrow a cup of sugar
- the neighbor two doors down whom you chat with for ten
  minutes on an evening walk but don't know super well—the
  people on social media you've met in real life a number of
  times but don't interact with much more than a quick like on
  a recent post.

There are other categories, of course, but we likely have similar categories of neighbors in our online spaces as well. Those
we follow on social media but don't know in real life, our friends

from college we've reconnected with but don't actually talk to anymore, our close friends and family that we engage with both on and off social media. Just like our physical world, our online neighbors fall into so many categories, and it's helpful to think about the range of depth we have in those relationships.

But what is so different about our online neighborhoods is, again, the ease at which we can interact with people we've never met or people we don't actually know well in real life. Our online communities can create a false sense of community—of people we don't actually know well. If you scroll through your social media right now, how many people do you follow that you've never met in person?

This has not always been the case; for many of us, using tools like Facebook began as a simple way to share photos and updates with friends and families. But over the years, social media and how we use it have both changed. Cal Newport, author of the book *Digital Minimalism*, describes the changes in social media this way: "Early social media focused on the behaviors that make people feel better: you would post things about yourself and check in/interact with your friends. Modern social media, which largely displaced the individual feed model with the algorithmically-generated timeline, instead emphasizes passive content consumption, as the amount of times you can check on your friends in a given week is relatively small, while the time you can dedicate to content consumption is boundless."[1] Going back to what we discussed in section 1 about the information landscape, what do those principles do to our sense of neighbor and who those people are?

Whom would you call your online neighbors? Or maybe a better question is, "Whom (or what) do you interact with regularly in your online spaces?" I suspect if we answer these questions honestly, we might surprise ourselves with our own answers. How many people do you actively engage with online or on social media? How many strangers do you follow? How many people are there whose content you consume but with whom don't actually interact? Christians talk a lot about loving our physical neighbors—bringing them meals, sharing a cup of sugar, having a backyard barbecue. But what does it look like to love our online neighbors? What's the online equivalent of talking over the fence? Consider taking a minute and making a list of some of your online neighbors. List the people you interact with intentionally and those whose content you passively consume. Notice who they are and how you know them.

I don't have all the answers, but if I honestly look at the amount of time I spend on social media and in online spaces, not much of that time is spent interacting with people I actually know. I spend a lot of time mindlessly scrolling through the content of creators I haven't actually met, and that kind of behavior is harder to fit into what it means to be a good online neighbor. If I follow only people I don't actually know, I don't really engage in any type of meaningful relationship. Don't get me wrong, lots of people create great content online around all sorts of topics— both educational and entertaining. I personally started creating content on Instagram to share my ideas, and most of the people following my account aren't people I've met.

But I also think it's helpful for us as we think about what it means to engage mindfully in our online spaces to at least notice how we spend our time and whom we follow and engage with. Like many things, there are no right or wrong answers about how you spend your time or who fills your social media feeds, but it's helpful for us to reflect on who these people are and the space they take up in our feeds and minds.

I'm grateful to be part of Mill City Church in Minneapolis, where we talk a lot about being present with our neighbors. We regularly talk about what it looks like to love our community in the name of Jesus. I love this outward focus because Mill City Church has been a part of some really great initiatives, from hosting a neighborhood Easter egg hunt to serving at the local food shelf to purposefully meeting in a local public school for worship instead of building a church building. All these things have been done in partnership with the local community. We talk regularly about how God is already at work in our neighborhoods, and we get to join him and his work.

But as we continue to spend more and more time online, what does it look like to believe that God might be at work in our online spaces? Our social media and our news feeds and our email? Do we listen for the Holy Spirit's promptings to know how to respond to the people in these spaces? Or like our day-to-day lives where we walk right past a neighbor down the street, when we're online, do we scroll by without pausing to think about how God might be prompting us? Are we mindless or mindful?

As we've talked about so many times already in this book, it's hard to be mindful and hard to pay attention to those promptings. We're human, after all. But those are exactly the things that can set us apart as people who follow Jesus. Choosing a different mindset allows us to behave differently and love others.

FOCUS ON RELATIONSHIPS

As I mentioned earlier, I've spent time overseas as a missionary and librarian. These experiences have been incredibly formative to how I view the world and how I've chosen to engage with other people. In 2015, my husband and I went to Uganda to work as librarian missionaries at a theological college for two months. We went to provide support and ideas around how the college could utilize their library to support their programs, as well as local pastors and community members. Since I had lived in Uganda before, I was eager to go back to a place that was so important to me. I had lived there before I was married and was also excited to go back with my husband so we could experience life in Uganda together.

Part of our onboarding process when we arrived in Uganda was to meet with various mission organization leaders, who helped us get settled. We had a number of great conversations that helped frame the two months we'd be in Uganda as we looked ahead to the time. One of the leaders gave us advice that we still come back to over and over even years later. He told us that if we wanted to have a lasting or kingdom impact during our time in Uganda, we should try to focus on doing three things:

1. Listen more.
2. Talk less.
3. Focus on relationships.

Although we had gone to Uganda to work in a library, he said that by focusing on these three things we'd have a greater impact than by simply trying to complete a checklist of to-dos in the library. He literally said that if we weren't willing to do these three things, we should pack our bags and go home, because we wouldn't have any kind of long-lasting, relational impact. This was similar to the lessons I had learned previously in my community development classes and time living overseas, but it was put so succinctly that it has stuck with me all these years later.

I don't think this leader was telling us that we'd never bring up hard topics while we were in Uganda or that as experts in our field of librarianship, we wouldn't offer advice to the college we were helping. But what my husband and I found so profound was that if we focused on people, we might have a better chance at actually making a difference in someone's life on a deeper, more personal level. In the end, we found this advice to be so true. We helped in the library, yes, and were able to offer some help and advice for ways to improve the library at the college. But most importantly, we were able to build friendships with people with whom we still email and text today.

Although these people were our physical neighbors only for a short time, they're now our online neighbors—people far away whom we still love and have relationships with. Our time in Uganda was about conveying information to a small group of people—offering a new set of eyes and making suggestions about their library. But the most impactful part of our time there wasn't about the library; it was about the meaningful relationships we created, despite our differences. It was about creating a partnership with the library and college staff and being culturally sensitive as we talked about the library.

I often wonder what it would look like to apply these principles to some of our current situations and divisions and to our online spaces that feel so overwhelming. Again, it's not to say we would or should never confront those who believe misinformation or have hard conversations. But what does it look like to put our relationships at the forefront of those conversations? It's not easy. Listening before speaking is hard! Focusing on relationships when we have strong opinions is incredibly difficult. We all have opinions and ideas and things we want to share. When we see or hear false information, we want to confront it. But we also have an opportunity to care about others.

In all the therapy I've attended over the years, my therapists have also always encouraged me to listen to others with curiosity or to listen for understanding, instead of getting upset or defensive right away. This advice has served me well in my marriage, at work, and in my friendships. When I listen to understand someone, just like the missions leader recommended, I'm able to see the other person for who they are, separate from their information consumption.

As we engage with people in our lives about all types of information—news, current events, and so on—we can have trouble separating the people from the information they consume. I'll admit, this can be incredibly challenging for me. Just like we talked about in the previous chapter, it's not hard for me to equate someone's news consumption with a lot of judgmental thoughts. If I'm willing to listen for understanding, I might have a better chance at separating the people I care about from the information they believe. I'm more able to model kindness before I engage in the hard conversations.

SPEAKING TRUTH AND BEING KIND

This might be the one thing I get asked about the most as I've engaged with the work of teaching people fact-checking skills in relation to their faith: How do I talk to people in my life who believe conspiracy theories? I've gotten emails from people telling me how their loved ones are caught in cycles of misinformation and disinformation about the 2020 election or the pandemic and asking how they can help their friends and family find better information. People in classes have brought up the conversations they have with their parents and siblings, and I hear the pain in their voices as they try to figure out how to love their family and friends and talk about the ways they disagree. Others talk about friends or colleagues at work and struggle to know how to engage the differences of opinions. Many times, they default to giving up, choosing to keep the peace as opposed to engaging with their loved ones with different opinions and beliefs.

I don't know whether I have tons of answers. I, too, have family and friends with whom I disagree on political and social issues. I believe some of them have fallen for misinformation—though they probably think the same about me! It can be very difficult to know how to move forward after we've done some fact-checking and thought through some issues. Like many people I know, I tend to keep quiet when I hear a loved one say something I think might be misinformation, choosing to keep the peace rather than engage. But there are some steps we can take and questions we can ask, because keeping quiet isn't always genuine peace. We're called to speak up, and I hope some of the thoughts in this chapter can help us all reflect on ways to move forward in kind ways, choosing to share truth even when it's hard. As we've said multiple times throughout this book, Satan loves when people believe lies, and we need to wrestle with how we'll share truth with others in order to be salt and light. We'll create only more division if we ignore the separations we experience.

A couple of years ago I went through a therapy program called dialectical behavioral therapy (DBT), as I mentioned in chapter 4. It's a structured therapy program, different from many cognitive therapy programs you may be familiar with, where I participated in a weekly therapist-led group meeting with others in the program, weekly individual meetings with my own therapist, along with filling out worksheets and homework. DBT focuses on a few main areas: mindfulness, distress tolerance, emotion regulation, and interpersonal effectiveness. All of the sections, or modules, work together to help participants live a life worth living. One of the skills taught in the interpersonal effectiveness module is a skill called "clarifying priorities" or "goals in interpersonal situations." While I was taught this skill in the context of therapy and my interpersonal relationships, I've found it to be invaluable in my online spaces as well.

This skill encourages participants to think about the goal or priority of an interaction beforehand to ensure they know what the focus will be while they're in the middle of a potentially difficult conversation or interpersonal situation. Sometimes the focus might change midconversation, but thinking about it ahead of time can help them stay on track. (Note: This is something for them to reflect on prior to a conversation, not something they need to announce to the other person at the beginning of a conversation.)

Three of the priorities mentioned that we might focus on are the following:

1. an objective—getting a result, something to change, or some-one to do something
2. the relationship—keeping and improving the relationship
3. your self-respect—respecting and expressing your own values and beliefs.

This tool has been incredibly helpful in a number of areas of my life. When I learned it, a light bulb went on. I realized I almost always had conversations that prioritized the relationship and that some of those conversations really needed to prioritize either an objective or my own self-respect. I've come back to this skill over and over and try to share it with others, because it can be helpful as we think about loving our neighbors both online and in person, especially when we talk about the news or other current events. We don't need to allow people to believe misinformation or disinformation, and being kind doesn't mean we always ignore our own opinions or needs for the sake of keeping the peace, but there are ways to do so lovingly. I've found that simply naming the objective in my mind before I start a conversation allows me to stay more focused during a conversation.

It's okay if the goal of a conversation is an objective, wanting something to change or for someone to do something. But it's important to clarify this for ourselves before we talk with someone. If the goal is getting something we want or wanting something to change, there are obviously loving ways to go about that conversation. There are also times where keeping a relationship is the most important goal, which means maybe we're more willing to compromise or let a comment go, even if we disagree. And sometimes, we need to hold on to our self-respect and express our own needs or values. In Christianese, this might also be called speaking the truth in love. I don't believe we need to let others continue to believe false information that might harm themselves or others. But how we go about expressing that might change in order to love them well.

How do we know what the priority should be? This is a perfect place to invite the Holy Spirit into another aspect of our online lives. Prayer might help us decide which of these priorities is the right one for the situation, the type of misinformation, and the relationship. This might sound basic and sort of like common sense, but again, if we want to be salt and light, shouldn't that include some reflection before we talk with others, asking the Holy Spirit for wisdom? If it's a particularly hard conversation, we might also invite trusted friends to pray with us or help us discern next steps. My husband and I have both sat with friends who asked us to intentionally help them discern next steps in relationships and other life events. We're part of the body of Christ for a reason—we need community! Before having hard conversations, we might ask the Holy Spirit for wisdom, but we might also ask others to help us discern how best to approach the conversation.

Another thing I've found helpful is an infographic from News Literacy Project called "How to Speak Up without Starting a Showdown" (shown here and listed in this chapter's resource list). News Literacy Project is a nonprofit organization working to provide tools and resources to both educators and the general public on issues surrounding misinformation. They provide education on how to identify misinformation and how to respond to it. In this particular infographic, they lay out some steps that can be helpful for talking with loved ones and keeping the conversations civil. The steps include things like finding common ground and determining whether the conversation should happen in public or private. It also mentions being patient, as conversations may need to happen over a span of time instead of just a one-and-done conversation. Once I talked through these principles in a class, and someone pointed out that the steps felt very in line with how Jesus might have responded to others. It was a good reminder that some of the best ways we can approach our loved ones are through the biblical, interpersonal skills we hopefully already use.

How to speak up without starting a showdown

Six best practices for talking to friends and family about sharing falsehoods online

News Literacy Project | checkology®

A future founded on facts
newslit.org checkology.org

1. Be civil

Use an empathetic and respectful tone. Avoid being judgmental or simply telling someone they are wrong. If a person replies with aggressive or sarcastic language, don't respond in kind.

2. Take your time

Firing off a knee-jerk response might be tempting, but pause and take a step back. Do your homework. Research the claim and find reputable fact-checking organizations or credible expert sources to share, which research shows is key to effectively correcting misinformation online.

> **Remember:** Two links are tougher to dismiss than one.

3. Find common ground

Try putting yourself in your friend or loved one's shoes. Why might they have posted this? Did they have good intentions? Consider pointing out shared concerns or feelings in your response.

> Misinformation exploits our beliefs and values to elicit an emotional reaction. But you can also focus on these underlying principles to establish your own good intentions in reaching out.

4. Lay out the facts

Rather than simply posting a link to a fact-check, clearly summarize the main findings of the debunk first, then add the link.

> Don't let the conversation get derailed by unwarranted attacks on fact-checking organizations. Leading with the evidence and sharing links to more than one fact-check example can help you avoid being drawn into a fight about the organization itself.

5. Public or private?

Decide how you want to post your response. Public comments can reach a bigger audience, but a private message may be more appropriate in some situations.

> **Tip:** Even if you opt for a private message, you can still leave a comment calling the original post into question (e.g., "Hmm. I'm not sure about this one.")

6. Be patient (and persistent)

Research shows we're more likely to believe fact-checks from people we know. View fact-checking as an ongoing debate rather than a fight to "win" at all costs. Even when someone seems unconvinced, calling out problematic content over time can plant a seed of doubt and prompt loved ones to work through important questions. While one corrective reply may not stop friends and relatives from sharing misinformation, consistently speaking up can help them think twice before sharing.

> **Remember:** Online trolls are not interested in honest debate. Don't waste your time responding to their insults or chasing their moving goalposts. Be willing to walk away.

Getting started: Some helpful phrases

> Oh, I saw this and initially thought it could be true, too. But ...

> Figuring out what's true online can be so overwhelming. But I did some digging and thought you'd want to know that it looks like this is misleading ...

> Hmm, this image/meme/article is kind of shocking, but I'm skeptical that it's real ...

> Do you know where this information came from? How did you find out about this?

> This image looks like it may not actually be what it seems. Here is a link to another version of the image, which shows something different. What do you think?

> I know we're all trying to be extra cautious because of all the bad information circulating on [insert subject]. Here is what I found ...

Resources consulted:

"What To Do If Your Family Or Friends Shares Misinformation On Facebook" (Brittany Wong, HuffPost).

"How to 'talk to friends and family about disinformation" (Claire Wardle, First Draft).

"PolitiFact: How to fact-check your friends and family on the coronavirus" (Daniel Funke, PolitiFact).

"Americans are fighting coronavirus misinformation on social media" (Leticia Bode and Emily Vraga, Washington Post).

"Opinion: How to Talk to Friends and Family Who Share Conspiracy Theories" (Charlie Warzel, The New York Times).

This infographic gives good advice for having hard conversations with others. Created by News Literacy Project. Used with permission.

So, what does it look like to be kind in our online spaces? Does it mean we just ignore what's going on or what our loved ones say? No, it doesn't. There are ways we can be kind and speak the truth.

In addition to my time with an individual therapist and in DBT, my husband and I have also pursued couples counseling in order to strengthen our marriage and repair old hurts. It's been invaluable, but that's a story for another time. Our couple's therapist often reminds us to "assume good intentions" about each other. And this is advice I've tried (emphasis on tried—no perfection here yet!) to adopt in other areas of my life. I try to assume people generally do the best they can. I've found that with my spouse, this is invaluable advice, but even with others in my world, it can be helpful to remember. Assuming people do the best they can and remembering that their opinions come from their own background and story give me empathy for them.

Don't get me wrong; it's hard. Throughout this book, I hope you've seen that we all evaluate information differently and see the world differently. It's hard to assume people do the best they can, especially if they deeply believe disinformation or conspiracy theories. But it seems to me that there's room to assume good intentions. What we see of other people's lives and opinions, especially on social media, is only one small piece of who they are and why they've landed with the opinions they have.

I think of this in my own life when I've found out that someone made assumptions about me that were wrong. I feel offended and a bit annoyed. Didn't they know that's not who I am? They didn't like something I said on a given day, but they didn't know it was a day I hadn't slept well and was dealing with some personal, family issues. I know that I want to be given the benefit of the doubt, so I'm learning to give it to others as well, even if I disagree with them.

THE GOAL

As we wrap up this chapter, I hope you'll find approaches to reflect on the ways in which you interact with people about information, whether they're people you see online or in your real life. We learn about the information landscape and fact-

checking so that we can start to find ways to share that information with others. It's not easy. I know how many times I avoid a
hard conversation. But we're not called to sit on the sidelines of
this world. We have an opportunity to take what we learn and
find ways of using it to love others better. Take a few minutes and
reflect on the people you interact with and whether your interactions are loving. Maybe journal, if that's your thing. Or pray over
your online spaces, asking God to help you be more loving. Take
the time to really reflect on what it means to love your neighbors
well—to live out your faith in your online spaces.

REFLECTION QUESTIONS

- When engaging with others online, will sharing an article
  or commenting on a friend's social media post, bring glory
  to the kingdom of God? For example, will you focus on the
  following:
  - loving others, lifting up the marginalized?
  - sharing truth with others, bringing peace to a situation
    or conversation?
- Can you tell when it might be better to have an in-person conversation with someone rather than sharing or posting online? (Hint: What would it look like to invite the Holy Spirit
  into your discernment?)
- If you disagree with something online or with something
  someone posted, how can you thoughtfully disagree in a way
  that invites dialogue, not arguing? How can you create space
  for dialogue that gets at the root of the topic or issue?
- How can you be an instrument of peace when you engage
  with others about news and current events, whether in person or online?
- Who are your online neighbors? How do you choose to interact with them? (See exercise 7.2.)

- How can you practice holding space for others' humanity while not holding space for the untrue things they believe?
- How can you practice kindness toward others while pointing them to the truth about current issues?
- Try naming your priorities before a hard conversation as described in the chapter. (See exercise 7.1.)

EXERCISE 7.1: CLARIFYING PRIORITIES

In this chapter, we talked about loving people well and that sometimes we still need to have difficult conversations with loved ones about misinformation or disinformation. This activity has been adapted from dialectical behavioral therapy (DBT) as a way for you to process before a conversation what your goal(s) might be for that interaction.

STEP 1. Think about an upcoming conversation that might be difficult. Think about what the conversation might be about.

STEP 2. As you think about having this conversation, note what you think your priority might be during the conversation:

- an objective—stating your opinion or need, or getting someone to do something
- the relationship—maintaining the relationship as the priority
- maintaining your self-respect—respecting your own values, acting in a way that you feel moral and capable.

STEP 3. Consider praying over the conversation ahead of time and over the priority you've chosen.

STEP 4. Have the conversation. Keep in mind the priority may change over the course of the conversation, and that's okay. You may even need to take a pause partway through the conversation.

Note: Obviously, if this is someone who is important to you, the relationship is always important. But sometimes the objective of a conversation needs to be about sharing a truth (in love) or being able to speak up against misinformation or share our own opinion or value.

STEP 5. After the conversation, journal or pray about how it went. What did you notice about trying to keep one of these priorities in your mind as you had the conversation? What did you learn about yourself?

For more information on this skill, try googling "DBT clarifying priorities." You'll find worksheets, podcasts, and YouTube videos. Although this exercise is generally taught as part of a therapy program, it has a lot to teach us about thinking about conversations prior to having them so that we can share truth in a more measured and calm way (as opposed to during an emotionally heated conversation). And as always, if you need therapy, reach out to a professional therapist for help. A DBT-trained therapist can also walk you through this exercise.

EXERCISE 7.2: WHO ARE YOUR ONLINE NEIGHBORS?

In this chapter we also talked about loving our online neighbors. But it can be helpful to reflect on who those people are that we interact with online. Who exactly are your online neighbors? This exercise will help you think through the people you regularly engage with and what steps you might want to take next, and reflect on how you interact with them.

STEP 1. Keep a log for a few days as you engage online or on social media (email counts too!), and write down some of the people you interact with online into two categories. First, list the people you know offline or in person but also interact with online. Second, list the people you don't actually know but follow on social media or watch online. Interactions with people in both lists may be passive (watching videos, absorbing content) or active (commenting, liking posts, etc.)

STEP 2. Look over your lists of people you know in real life but also interact with online. Reflect on the following questions: Do you interact with these people online because they live far away and that's how you keep in touch? Or do you interact with them online because it's easier to simply like or comment on a post than have an in-person conversation with them.

STEP 3. Now look over the list of people you follow or interact with but don't actually know in real life. Why do you follow them? Do you actively consume their content, or do you mindlessly scroll through it?

STEP 4. Reflect on both lists of people and the content you follow and interact with. What themes do you notice? What promptings do you notice? How might you want to change how you interact with your online neighbors?

ADDITIONAL RESOURCES

Braver Angels. https://braverangels.org/. This organization focuses on facilitating conversations among people from different political viewpoints with the goal of depolarization and bringing people together who may have different viewpoints. They offer online workshops and classes, as well as events in local communities. Jesus modeled for us the importance of eating with people and spending time with people that others would have avoided (e.g., tax collectors). Although not a Christian organization, Braver Angels facilitates the same thing—opportunities for us to sit down and have a conversation with someone who might live or think differently than we do. Although this organization focuses on pol-

itics and I focus more broadly on information, there's a lot for us
to learn from having more productive conversations, whether of
a political nature or not.

Cho, Eugene. *Thou Shalt Not Be a Jerk*. Colorado Springs: David C.
Cook, 2020. Again, this book has a lot to say about having productive conversations with loved ones. Although focused on politics,
there are helpful things that can inform our conversations and
how we engage with information, since so much of the information we seek is political or has political bias.

"How to Have Conversations with People Who Hate You? (with Dylan
Marron)." In *How to Be a Better Human*. Podcast audio. September 20, 2021. https://open.spotify.com/episode/1jQnF8PfdpYKo9J
guhinlc?si=jQRXTrTHQNmGh2XSVoI7kg. This podcast includes
an interview with Dylan Marron, who reaches out to those who
have said negative comments about him online and then has a
conversation with them. He reminds us that the people on the
other side of the screen are also human beings with their own
stories. There are some great reminders here about how honest,
real conversations make a big difference in our relationships and
breaking down barriers.

"How to Speak Up without Starting a Showdown." Infographic. News
Literacy Project. https://newslit.org/wp-content/uploads/2020/12
/How-to-speak-up-without-starting-a-showdown.pdf. This infographic outlines some steps you can take to talk with loved ones
who believe misinformation, while being kind. A participant in
one of my classes noted that many of the steps listed in this infographic feel very much like things Jesus would have done.

Skills for Social Media. https://braverangels.org/what-we-do/skills
-for-social-media/. A free online course from Braver Angels that
will help you avoid polarization in your social media and engage
more productively with differences. This course is something you
can do at your own pace.

Conclusion

So here we are. We've covered a lot of ground. From the big picture of the information landscape to the nitty-gritty of researching specific claims you see online. Finally, we've thought about how we engage with others after we've done our own fact-checking work.

How do you feel? (Yes, those emotions again!) I hope you're less overwhelmed than when you started this book, but I also know it can be a lot to digest. Maybe you, like some people, feel more overwhelmed because you know more than you did before. I'd encourage you to think about each section like another piece of the puzzle to help you understand our world a bit more. Like I said in the introduction, the goal of the last seven chapters wasn't to change your political ideologies or to make you scared of social media and the internet.

The goal is to give you tools to be more intentional in your online spaces. As you look ahead to the next time you open your phone and scroll through the news or social media, I hope you find ways to bring intentionality to those spaces. I hope instead of mindlessly scrolling, you'll mindfully and purposefully seek opportunities to build relationships and be salt and light online, sharing truth and kindness.

PRACTICAL LAST STEPS

Remember, it takes practice and experimenting. Try different fact-checking tools in different scenarios. Try approaching your loved ones differently when you want to talk about a current issue or important topic. Try reading different news sources, and see how they talk about the issues. As the saying goes, nothing changes if nothing changes. It might be awkward at first, but at least you may get a different result and learn something about yourself or someone else. So make a commitment to change one thing, and slowly you'll find yourself in new online spaces and maybe even discovering new ways to engage.

As I said in the introduction, my church practices many experiments as we learn new ways of engaging with our community. I've found this idea of experimentation to be a helpful framework in so many areas of my life. At our church, the experiments might be about trying a new way to engage with our neighborhood or exploring new ways to connect with social injustices in our city. This mentality allows us to try things without worrying about the outcome. The church leadership encourages us to try new ways of loving our neighbors, reflect on how things went, and see where God might lead us. We often couple this with the spiritual practice of dwelling in the word (where we sit with one Bible passage for a while, meditating on it and listening to the Spirit) or listening prayer (where we spend a lot of time listening to the Spirit before praying). These practices allow our experiments to be rooted in our faith as we reach out in new ways to our neighbors.

Similarly, in other areas of our lives—and in this case, our on-line lives—we might have a sense that we need to make a change but aren't sure what that change is. Instead of trying to chart out the next five steps of an unknown change, try experimenting by taking one step and then reflecting on it. What does the experiment stir up in you? If you haven't already, use the exercises or reflection questions at the end of each chapter to help you experiment with different ways of engaging if you need some ideas. The freeing thing about experiments is that if they don't work, you can try something else! Or try them again. And either way, you'll probably learn something—about yourself, about your faith, about the online environment.

A FINAL BLESSING

Two years ago, as I wrapped up a series of Faith and Fake News classes at my church, a friend said something in the last class that has stuck with me ever since. She said that all this content— how to fact-check, how to talk with loved ones, algorithms, the information landscape, and so on—is where the rubber meets the road of our faith. She said some of us want to simply be sheep who sit patiently at the feet of the Shepherd, learning from him and listening to his voice. But we're called to move out into the world, to engage with others, to help the hurting, and to be a part of his justice-bringing kingdom. For some of us, this is the hard part: the action part of our faith. Maybe our personality is more contemplative, or maybe we just find it more comfortable to practice other aspects of living out our faith, like prayer or reading our Bibles. But choosing to seek truth in our online spaces, engage with it, learn from it, and share truth with others is all part of God's redemptive work in our world. Our faith is lived out in so many ways, and hopefully you see the ways in which you can take your faith into your online spaces.

My prayer for you has never been that you'll fact-check everything you see, read, or hear. My prayer for everyone who reads this book is that you'll bring a spirit of grace and kindness to your online spaces. That you'll learn to discern what's true and be humble enough to recognize when you get it wrong. That you'll find ways to proclaim truth and to speak up against areas you see that are unjust or untrue. And most importantly, my prayer for you is that you'll approach your online spaces a bit more like Jesus: with love for your neighbors as you share truth.

And ultimately, as you do this work, as you become more like Jesus in how you interact with information and people, I hope you'll also remember that we already know the end of the story. We can see the division around us and know that Jesus wins in the end. That's not to say we should be arrogant and prideful and ignore these things. But we can have hope that he's on his throne and that his truth ultimately wins.

I'll leave you with one last set of verses as we wrap up these lessons, Colossians 3:12–17:

> [12]Therefore, as God's chosen people, holy and dearly loved, clothe yourselves with compassion, kindness, humility, gentleness and patience. [13]Bear with each other and forgive one another if any of you has a grievance against someone. Forgive as the Lord forgave you. [14]And over all these virtues put on love, which binds them all together in perfect unity. [15]Let the peace of Christ rule in your hearts, since as members of one body you were called to peace. And be thankful. [16]Let the message of Christ dwell among you richly as you teach and admonish one another with all wisdom through psalms, hymns, and songs from the Spirit, singing to God with gratitude in your hearts. [17]And whatever you do, whether in word or deed, do it all in the name of the Lord Jesus, giving thanks to God the Father through him. (NIV)

These verses remind us that we're all connected, part of the church. Learning to do this work in our online spaces isn't only about our individual truth-seeking but also about being a part of something bigger than ourselves—about pursuing the fruit of the Spirit not just with people at work, in our neighborhood, or in our homes but also in the ways we interact online. It's not easy, and it takes lots of practice. Sometimes, these verses feel unattainable to me. I don't always want to be patient with others or forgive them or love them well, especially when I see the things they post online. But as I said in the beginning, the hard things in life are almost always the ones I find worth doing.

So, as we finish these conversations, may you be blessed with wisdom as you navigate your online spaces. May you be blessed with patience as you navigate hard conversations with your loved ones. May you be blessed with the ability to find ways to share the truth. And may you be blessed with perseverance to love others well and to continue to seek humility and truth, even when it's hard. It's in those moments you'll become more like Jesus.

REFLECTION QUESTIONS

- How will you practice some of the skills mentioned throughout this book? With specific kinds of information? Or when using specific apps or under certain circumstances? Consider naming some specific things you can practice regularly and sharing them with someone you trust to hold you accountable.
- What will you do differently going forward? Make a plan, and share it with a friend who can hold you accountable.
- Throughout the chapters, where have you sensed the Holy Spirit's prompting to be more intentional online?
- What does it look like to sit at the feet of Jesus and learn from him and then take what you learn into your online spaces? How will you wear your faith lens first when consuming information?

Acknowledgments

I can't finish this book without thanking the people who helped me throughout the last few years, as I explored the intersection of faith and misinformation.

Many thanks to all the class participants at Mill City Church, who were my guinea pigs as I started exploring these ideas. And especially thanks to Pastor Stephanie O'Brien, who gave me the opportunity to offer the first Faith and Fake News class.

I am also grateful to the other churches that took a chance on me and allowed me to share these concepts with their congregations. I've learned so much from all of you, and many of these concepts continue to be refined by our conversations.

Thank you to the media outlets and content creators who have highlighted this work over the past few years, including those from Minnesota Public Radio, Business Insider, Love Thy Neighborhood Podcast, The Holy Post Podcast, and The Two Cities Podcast. Thank you for helping me spread the word about the importance of this work for Christians.

Thanks to the friends who read drafts of this book and offered ideas to make it relevant and clear and to all the friends who kindly let me cancel plans on them while I was writing.

Finally, many, many thanks to my husband, Brian, who has been a constant sounding board and encourager. Thanks for reading countless drafts of this book and processing this content over and over with me. Most importantly, thanks for believing in me.

Notes

Part One

1. "Infodemic," World Health Organization, https://www.who.int/health-topics/infodemic.

Chapter 1

1. *Merriam-Webster*, s.v. "algorithm," https://www.merriam-webster.com/dictionary/algorithm.
2. *Merriam-Webster*, s.v. "filter bubble," https://www.merriam-webster.com/dictionary/filter%20bubble.
3. Eli Pariser, "Beware Online Filter Bubbles," TED video, March 2011, https://www.ted.com/talks/eli_pariser_beware_online_filter_bubbles/transcript?language=en.

Chapter 2

1. IDC and Statista, "Volume of Data/Information Created, Captured, Copied, and Consumed Worldwide from 2010 to 2025 (in

Zettabytes)," chart, June 7, 2021, Statista, https://www.statista.com
/statistics/871513/worldwide-data-created/.

Chapter 4

1. "Ledger of Harms," Center for Humane Technology, https://
ledger.humanetech.com/#study_128.
2. Mike Caulfield, *Web Literacy for Student Fact-Checkers* (self-
pub., 2017), chapter 3, https://webliteracy.pressbooks.com/chapter
/building-a-habit-by-checking-your-emotions/.
3. Stephanie Preston, Anthony Anderson, David J. Robertson,
Mark P. Shephard, and Narisong Huhe, "Detecting Fake News on
Facebook: The Role of Emotional Intelligence," *PLOS ONE* 16, no. 3
(2021): e0246757, https://doi.org/10.1371/journal.pone.0246757.

Chapter 5

1. "Fact Check—Facebook Has Not Banned 'the Lord's Prayer,'"
Reuters Fact Check, January 17, 2022, https://www.reuters.com/arti
cle/factcheck-facebook-prayer/fact-check-facebook-has-not-banned
-the-lords-prayer-idUSL1N2TX1HF.
2. Eric Lendrum, "Antifa Rioters Deface World War II and Lincoln
Memorials on National Mall," American Greatness, June 1, 2020,
https://amgreatness.com/2020/06/01/antifa-rioters-deface-world-war
-ii-and-lincoln-memorials-on-national-mall/.
3. *Merriam-Webster*, s.v. "bias," https://www.merriam-webster
.com/dictionary/bias.
4. Bettina J. Casad, "Confirmation Bias," *Encyclopaedia Britannica*,
October 9, 2019, https://www.britannica.com/science/confirmation
-bias.
5. Eli Pariser, *The Filter Bubble* (New York: Penguin, 2011), 88.
6. Linda Skitka (Moral Combat), interview with Shankar Vedantam, *Hidden Brain*, podcast audio, October 19, 2020, https://hidden
brain.org/podcast/moral-combat/.

7. Amy Mitchell et al., "Distinguishing between Factual and Opinion Statements in the News," Pew Research Center, June 18, 2018, https://www.pewresearch.org/journalism/2018/06/18/distinguishing-between-factual-and-opinion-statements-in-the-news/.

8. Eryn Roles, Kathleen Phillips, and Sabrina Thomas, "IF I APPLY—a Source Evaluation Tool: Home," https://libguides.marshall.edu/IFIAPPLY.

Chapter 6

1. Howard Thurman, *Meditations of the Heart* (Boston: Beacon, 1981), 189–90.

2. *Merriam-Webster*, s.v. "humble," https://www.merriam-webster.com/dictionary/humble.

3. Eugene Cho, *Thou Shalt Not Be a Jerk* (Colorado Springs: David C. Cook, 2020), 17.

4. Adam Grant, *Think Again: The Power of Knowing What You Don't Know* (New York: Viking, 2021), 54.

Chapter 7

1. Cal Newport, "Social Media's Shift toward Misery," *Study Hacks Blog*, December 13, 2019, https://www.calnewport.com/blog/2019/12/13/social-medias-shift-toward-misery/.

Bibliography

Casad, Bettina J. "Confirmation Bias." *Encyclopaedia Britannica*. October 9, 2019. https://www.britannica.com/science/confirmation-bias.

Caulfield, Mike. *Web Literacy for Student Fact-Checkers*. Self-published, 2017. https://webliteracy.pressbooks.com/.

Center for Humane Technology. "Ledger of Harms." https://ledger.humanetech.com/#study_128.

Cho, Eugene. *Thou Shalt Not Be a Jerk*. Colorado Springs: David C. Cook, 2020.

Grant, Adam. *Think Again: The Power of Knowing What You Don't Know*. New York: Viking, 2021.

IDC and Statista. "Volume of Data/Information Created, Captured, Copied, and Consumed Worldwide from 2010 to 2025 (in Zetta-bytes)." Chart. June 7, 2021. Statista. https://www.statista.com/statistics/871513/worldwide-data-created/.

Lendrum, Eric. "Antifa Rioters Deface World War II and Lincoln Memorials on National Mall." American Greatness. June 1, 2020. https://amgreatness.com/2020/06/01/antifa-rioters-deface-world-war-ii-and-lincoln-memorials-on-national-mall/.

Mitchell, Amy, Jeffrey Gottfried, Michael Barthel, and Nami Sumida. "Distinguishing between Factual and Opinion Statements in the News." Pew Research Center. June 18, 2018. https://www.pewresearch.org/journalism/2018/06/18/distinguishing-between-factual-and-opinion-statements-in-the-news/.

Newport, Cal. "Social Media's Shift toward Misery." *Study Hacks Blog.* December 13, 2019. https://www.calnewport.com/blog/2019/12/13/social-medias-shift-toward-misery/.

Pariser, Eli. *The Filter Bubble: How the New Personalized Web Is Changing What We Read and How We Think.* New York: Penguin, 2011.

———. "Beware Online Filter Bubbles." TED video. March 2011. https://www.ted.com/talks/eli_pariser_beware_online_filter_bubbles/transcript?language=en.

Preston, Stephanie, Anthony Anderson, David J. Robertson, Mark P. Shephard, and Narisong Huhe. "Detecting Fake News on Facebook: The Role of Emotional Intelligence." *PLOS ONE* 16, no. 3 (2021): e0246757. https://doi.org/10.1371/journal.pone.0246757.

Reuters Fact Check. "Fact Check—Facebook Has Not Banned 'the Lord's Prayer.'" January 17, 2022. https://www.reuters.com/article/factcheck-facebook-prayer/fact-check-facebook-has-not-banned-the-lords-prayer-idUSL1N2TX1HF.

Roles, Eryn, Kathleen Phillips, and Sabrina Thomas. "IF I APPLY—a Source Evaluation Tool: Home." https://libguides.marshall.edu/IFIAPPLY.

Skitka, Linda (Moral Combat). Interview with Shankar Vedantam. *Hidden Brain.* Podcast audio. October 19, 2020. https://hiddenbrain.org/podcast/moral-combat/.

Thurman, Howard. *Meditations of the Heart.* Boston: Beacon, 1981.

World Health Organization. "Infodemic." https://www.who.int/health-topics/infodemic.

Index